A CHILD IN WINTER

A CHILD IN WINTER

ADVENT, CHRISTMAS, AND EPIPHANY WITH

CARYLL HOUSELANDER

✳ ✳ ✳

EDITED WITH SCRIPTURE SELECTIONS AND COMMENTS BY
THOMAS HOFFMAN

Sheed & Ward
Franklin, Wisconsin

Sheed & Ward Ltd.
4 Rickett Street
London SW6 1RU

As an apostolate of the Priests of the Sacred Heart, a Catholic religious congregation, the mission of Sheed & Ward is to publish books of contemporary impact and enduring merit in Catholic Christian thought and action. The books published, however, reflect the opinion of their authors and are not meant to represent the official position of the Priests of the Sacred Heart.

	2000	
Sheed & Ward		Sheed & Ward Ltd.
7373 South Lovers Lane Road		4 Rickett Street
Franklin, Wisconsin 53132		London SW6 1RU
1-800-266-5564		ISBN 0 7220 1751 0

Selections from *The Reed of God* (1954), *The Risen Christ* (1958), *The Passion of the Infant Christ* (1953), *The Comforting of Christ* (1947) Copyright © Caryll Houselander and used with the permission of Sheed & Ward. In these selections, punctuation has been standardized and the text has been rendered gender inclusive.

Comments Copyright © 2000 by Thomas Hoffman

Scripture quotations are from the New Revised Standard Version of the Bible, copyright 1989 by the Division of Christian Education of the National Council of the Churches of Christ in the USA. Used by permission. All rights reserved.

Printed in the United States of America

Cover and interior design by Madonna Gauding
Cover art by Ansgar Holmberg, CSJ. Used with Permission.

Library of Congress Cataloging-in-Publication Data

Houselander, Caryll.
  A child in winter : Advent, Christmas, and Epiphany with Caryll Houselander /
  Edited, with Scripture selections and comments by Thomas Hoffman.
    p. cm.
  Includes bibliographical references.
  ISBN 1-58051-085-X (pbk. : alk. paper)
    1.   Advent—Meditations. 2. Christmas—Meditations. 3. Epiphany—
        Meditations.
    4. Devotional calendars. I. Hoffman, Thomas. II. Title.

BV40 .H67 2000
242'.33—dc21

                                                            00-035770

1 2 3 4 5 / 03 02 01 00

To Michael and Our Lady

Contents

✳ ✳ ✳

1
INTRODUCTION

5
FIRST WEEK OF ADVENT

27
SECOND WEEK OF ADVENT

49
THIRD WEEK OF ADVENT

69
FEASTS AND DAYS IN ADVENT

99
FEASTS AND DAYS IN CHRISTMAS

137
FEASTS AND DAYS IN EPIPHANY

INTRODUCTION

CARYLL HOUSELANDER was a laywoman, mystic, and poet whose timeless vision of spiritual childhood comforted and challenged the English-speaking world through the ravages of World War II and the London Blitz. An artist, woodcarver, and liturgical designer, Houselander's vision of God as Father and Mother was deeply grounded in Scripture, the people of God, ordinary life around her, and her own intimate union with Christ, Our Lady, and the saints. Her spiritual imagination is communal, and she consistently directs us to Christ by way of showing hospitality to strangers.

True to Houselander's vision and witness, this companion through the seasons reflects our high, baptismal calling to service and personal transformation. Houselander reminds us that now is not the time for shallow sentimentality. Rather, this is the Advent of our salvation—our invitation to prepare, to welcome, and to honor God who grows in our midst and the Spirit who is poured out on all flesh.

In winter the frozen earth lies fallow, but God is pleased to warm us with Christ's presence. Every year the rhythm repeats through the favored seasons of Advent,

Christmas, and Epiphany. Every year God's promise is planted, takes root, and grows large—renewing our youth and causing Light to transform the darkness. In that renewal, Houselander calls us to be attentive to our mystical connection to one another. One day, a friend found her prostrated on the ground in a shed:

"Caryll, are you ill?" she asked.

"No, but a friend of mine is going through a fierce temptation and I must suffer it with her," she answered. For it is not only material help that Christ desires to give through human hands. For we are all one and

"We are only syllables
Of the perfect Word."[1]

Caryll Houselander was keenly aware of her spiritual connection with other people. This collection invites you to share with her the joy of the Child in Winter—the Christ who comes forth as Salvation, drawn deep from the well of our shared humanity. Informed and inspired by Houselander's rich legacy, and with her as your companion and guide, *A Child in Winter* invites you, even in the midst of winter, to grow large with the presence and love of God.

1. *Caryll Houselander: That Divine Eccentric* by Maisie Ward. Sheed & Ward: New York, 1962. p.136

The time of Advent is absolutely essential to our contemplation.
If we have truly given our humanity to be changed into Christ,
it is essential to us that we do not disturb this time of growth.

✳ ✳ ✳

It is a time of darkness, of faith.
We shall not see Christ's radiance in our lives yet;
it is still hidden in our darkness; nevertheless, we must believe
that he is growing in our lives; we must believe it so firmly
that we cannot help relating everything, literally everything,
to this almost incredible reality.

(The Reed of God, p. 29)

First Week of Advent

SUNDAY

The Habit of Advent

The apostles gathered around Jesus, and told him all that they had done and taught. He said to them, "Come away to a deserted place all by yourselves and rest a while."

—Mark 6:30–31

THERE IS GREAT VIRTUE in practicing patience in small things until the habit of Advent returns to us. Sometimes this Advent season of the soul is a recurring rhythm through life, deliberately chosen as such or simply given to us. Sometimes it is the immediate result of conversion or of a new awareness of God or of an increase of Love.

Sometimes it is a painful experience. It may be that a soul brimmed with love becomes dumb, inarticulate, blind, seeing only darkness, unable to give things that it longs to give to a world of children asking for bread.

That simply means that the Holy Spirit of Love, by which Christ was conceived in the heart, is compelling it to suffer the period of growth. The light is shining in the darkness, but the darkness does not comprehend it.

To a soul in such a condition, peace will come as soon as it turns to Our Lady and imitates her. In her the Word of God chose to be silent for the season measured by God. She, too, was silent; in her the light of the world shone in darkness. Today, in many souls, Christ asks that he may grow secretly, that he may be the light shining in the darkness.

In the seasons of our Advent—waking, working, eating, sleeping, being—each breath is a breathing of Christ into the world.

(*The Reed of God*, p. 38)

* * *

STANDING AT THE THRESHOLD of another Advent we hear the invitation of Christ: "Come away to a deserted place and rest a while." And so we begin our season of growth and expectation—a time to secret ourselves with Mary, to join our hearts with hers, and to grow pregnant with God together. God invites us to a quiet place of reflection and bounty. This Advent, choose some time for silence. Make space within yourself to grow large with the abundance of God's favor. Make this a time to fill your lungs deeply with God so that you can breathe Christ into the world.

* * *

O GOD WHO HAS SUMMONED US, give strength to your people this Advent so that we may rise up and fearlessly walk with you in deserted places and find rest.

MONDAY

Giving Christ Life in Us

Thus says the Lord GOD, Alas for the senseless prophets who follow their own spirit, and have seen nothing! Your prophets have been like jackals among ruins.

—Ezekiel 13:3–4

STRANGELY ENOUGH, those who complain the loudest of the emptiness of their lives are usually people whose lives are overcrowded, filled with trivial details, plans, desires, ambitions, unsatisfied cravings for passing pleasures, doubts, anxieties and fears; and these sometimes are further overlaid with exhausting pleasures which are an attempt, and always a futile attempt, to forget how pointless such people's lives are. Those who complain in these circumstances of the emptiness of their lives are usually afraid to allow space or silence or pause in their lives. They dread space, for they want material things crowded together, so that there will always be something to lean on for support. They dread silence, because they do not want to hear their own pulses beating out the seconds of their life, and to know that each beat is another knock on the door of death.

They have no sense of being related to any abiding beauty, to any indestructible life: they are afraid to be alone with their unrelated hearts.

Our own effort will consist in sifting and sorting out everything that is not essential and that fills up space and silence in us and in discovering what sort of shape this emptiness in us is. From this we shall learn what sort of purpose God has for us. In what way are we to fulfill the work of giving Christ life in us?
(*The Reed of God,* pp. 2–3)

* * *

ADVENT is a season of silence and rest with God. But in silence we sometimes feel meaningless, like prophets who have seen nothing. But does God ever truly hide from us, or have we struck out on our own only to find ourselves ultimately misplaced, spending our time and energy chasing after shadows in the ruins? If we have lost a sense of beauty and wonder, has God ceased to be beautiful, or have we blazed paths of our own and gotten lost along the way—losing our connections to our community, our neighbor, and our God? Take time to focus and examine your conscience. What is the shape of your empty ruin? How are you still connected to God's abiding beauty? This Advent, how will you fulfill the work of giving Christ life?

*　*　*

O GOD WHO IS EVER-PRESENT, rescue us from
the ruins and keep us from distraction this Advent,
so that in simplicity of heart we may see your beauty.

TUESDAY

The Advent of Our Contemplation

God's love for Israel:
"I led them with cords of human kindness,
*   with bands of love.*
I was to them like those
*   who lift infants to their cheeks.*
I bent down to them and fed them."

—Hosea 11:4

WHEN A WOMAN is carrying a child she develops a certain instinct of self-defense. It is not selfishness; it is not egoism. It is an absorption into the life within, a folding of self like a little tent around the child's frailty, a God-like instinct to cherish, and some day to bring forth the life. A closing upon it like the petals of a flower closing upon the dew that shines in its heart.

This is precisely the attitude we must have to Christ, the Life within us, in the Advent of our contemplation.

We could scrub the floor for a tired friend, or dress a wound for a patient in a hospital, or lay the table and wash up for the family; but we shall not do it in martyr spirit or with that worse spirit of self-congratulation, of feeling that we are making *ourselves* more perfect, more unselfish, more positively kind.

We shall do it for just one thing, that our hands make Christ's hands in our life, that our service may let Christ serve through us, that our patience may bring Christ's patience back to the world.

By his own will Christ was dependent on Mary during Advent: he was absolutely helpless; he could go nowhere but where she chose to take him; he could not speak; her breathing was his breath; his heart beat in the beating of her heart.

Today Christ is dependent upon us. This dependence of Christ lays a great trust upon us. During this tender time of Advent we must carry him in our hearts to wherever he wants to go, and there are many places to which he may never go unless we take him.
(*The Reed of God*, pp. 30–31)

✳   ✳   ✳

TO SERVE means that we bend ourselves low—crushing our ego and bending our pride in compassion for another. When we contemplate, we fold ourselves small and place our thoughts in the service of another—losing awareness of self to make space for the reality of God. In either case—to serve or to contemplate—we abandon selfish interests. Not as if our interests and self-worth are meaningless, but we let go of them to make a gift of them for another—a valuable and precious gift. God has bent down to us. The fullness of God has been folded small and placed inside of us. When we fold in upon ourselves and contemplate or in humility serve the gift of God in our neighbor, we are not becoming less ourselves. We are becoming more like God.

* * *

O GOD WHO HAS BENT DOWN TO US, help us to contemplate and to pray this Advent, so that our service of others will be a true gift of self, and of love.

WEDNESDAY

Christ Shall Come to Us in Everyone

For the LORD your God is God of gods and Lord of lords, the great God, mighty and awesome, who is not partial and takes no bribe, who executes justice for the orphan and the widow, and who loves the strangers, providing them food and clothing.

—Deuteronomy 10:17–18

IT IS PART OF GOD'S PLAN for us that Christ shall come to us in everyone; it is in their particular role that we must learn to know him. He may come as a little child, making enormous demands, giving enormous consolation. He may come as a stranger, so that we must give the hospitality to a stranger that we should like to give to Christ. He may come to us in his Passion, disfigured by our sins and all sin, asking the utmost courage of us, that we may not be scandalized and may believe. He may come to us as a servant and compel us to the extreme of humility which accepts his service, as Peter had to do, when he washed his feet, and as the disciples did with unquestioning joy, when he cooked their little meal on the seashore.

If we see everyone in our life as "another Christ" we shall treat everyone with the reverence and objectivity

that must grow into love and, as a matter of sheer logic, we shall accept whatever they bring to us, in the way of joy or sorrow or responsibility, as coming from the hand of Christ; and because nothing comes from his hand that is not given for our ultimate happiness, we shall gradually learn that the things they do, the demands they make, are all part of God's plan for us. Once that is understood we can never again feel completely frustrated by anyone, or lose the serenity of our minds by nursing a grievance. Neither shall we ever again miss a joy that should have been ours through another person because we dared not give ourselves to it bravely.
(*The Risen Christ*, pp. 32–33)

* * *

WE ARE ACCUSTOMED to economic and scientific objectivity. Flesh-and-blood human beings are handled as ciphers on actuarial tables—"taxpayers," "consumers," "users." We evaluate and rank based on productivity and habit—keeping accounts of what we *do* and losing sight of who we really *are*. Our alternative to this dehumanizing, scientific, and economic objectivity is not sentimentality or shapeless love. It is an objective love—a dispassionate passion. It is the passion of God for all people—regardless of habit or custom, race or disposition, gender or economic status. It is a daring and brave position, but it is one that sides with God who stretches our hearts and minds this Advent to see the stranger, the dispossessed, and the outcast, and challenges us to love.

✳ ✳ ✳

O GOD WHO WELCOMES STRANGERS, enlarge and warm the cavern of our hearts this Advent so that we may welcome and cherish all people as gifts offered to us by you.

THURSDAY

Formed into Christ

*In the beginning, when God created the heavens and the earth,
the earth was a formless void and darkness covered the face of the
deep, while a wind from God swept over the face of the waters.*

—Genesis 1:1–2

WHILE CHRIST remained hidden in Mary, his rest was a tremendous activity; he was making her into himself, making himself from her. From her eyes he was making the eyes that would weep over Jerusalem, that would shine upon the wildflowers, that would close in death and open in the morning of Resurrection. From her hands he was making the hands that would heal and raise the dead and be nailed to the cross. From her heart he was making the heart whose love would redeem the world.

The same thing happens when, allowing the Infant Christ to rest in us, we wait patiently on his own timing of his growth in us, and give him just what he asks, the extremely simple things that are ourselves—our hands and feet, our eyes and ears, our words, our thoughts, our love. Not only does he grow in us, but we are formed into him.

(*The Passion of the Infant Christ*, pp. 23–24)

*   *   *

IN THE BEGINNING, the Spirit brooded over the face of the waters and God spoke and there was Light. Likewise, in the fullness of time, an angel announced to Mary and the same creative Spirit visited her and she conceived the Son of God. This Advent, *our* Advent, is equally a time of creation. God's same Spirit abides in us—brooding over our waters—shaping and forming us, being formed and shaped by us. We are God's creative works in process. God alone knows what we shall become. What might God have in store in the fullness of *our* time? In the beginning, God created Light. In Mary, God became flesh. What will God become in us this Advent? Is there room in us for God's seed to take root and grow? God has visited us with grace and favor. Are we ready to become Light?

*   *   *

O GOD OF WONDERS, you called Light into being and manifested your glory in Mary's womb. This Advent, fill us with your Spirit and make us Light.

FRIDAY

Love Is More Effective Than Words

Love does no wrong to a neighbor; therefore, love is the fulfilling of the law.

—Romans 13:10

T HE STORY of Joseph's bewilderment when he realized that his future wife was going to have a baby is well known, and it is well known, too, that Our Lady did not explain.

Her example here teaches us wisdom, when misunderstandings arise because of Christ conceived in us. There is little gained by trying to explain. At that time, the Advent time, God's voice is silent in us; it is simply our own heartbeat. Love is more effective than words.

The only thing to do is to go on loving, to be patient, to suffer the misunderstanding. Explanations even of what *can* be explained seldom heal—and there is so much that cannot be explained.

Even the presence of Christ in us does not do away with our own clumsiness, blindness, stupidity; indeed, sometimes because of *our* limitations, his light is a blinding light to us and we become, for a time, more dense than before. We shall still be irritable, still make mistakes, and still very likely be unaware of how exasperating we are.

Explanations, words, at this stage, may only wound, but love will be a bridge over which at last, in God's time, we shall cross to a better understanding. (*The Reed of God*, pp. 17–18)

✳ ✳ ✳

JOSEPH HAD A VISION, but no explanation. Mary had an angelic conversation and was overshadowed by the power of the Most High, but she didn't have an instruction manual or theological essay to increase her understanding. Still, Mary and Joseph shared two things: love and trust. They loved and trusted God and one another. They had hearts and lives that were open to mysterious visitors and poetic ambiguity. Mary heard the angel's announcement of God's high favor, and heard God's invitation to have an especially abundant share of God's grace. Astonished and surprised, without reading any of the small print, Our Lady answered in faith: "Here am I, the servant of the Lord." Joseph, visited by a somewhat ambiguous angel in the mists of a dream, trusted and believed. No proofs, lawyers, or guarantees, just love and trust shared in silence. Could that ever be enough for us?

*   *   *

O GOD OF TRUTH AND CONSTANT FIDELITY, make us bold this Advent so that, like Mary and Joseph, we may trust and love without question.

Saturday

Expensive People

For the grace of God has appeared, bringing salvation to all, training us to renounce impiety and worldy passions, and in the present age to live lives that are self-controlled, upright, and godly, while we wait for the blessed hope and the manifestation of the glory of our great God and Savior, Jesus Christ.

—Titus 2:11–13

THE EXPENSIVE PEOPLE are those who, because they are not simple, make complicated demands—people to whom we cannot respond spontaneously and simply, without anxiety. They need not be abnormal to exact these complicated responses; it is enough that they should be untruthful or touchy or hypersensitive or that they have an exaggerated idea of their own importance or that they have a pose—one which may have become second nature but is not what they really are. With all such people we are bound to experience a little hitch in our response. In time, our relationship with them becomes unreal. If we have to consider every word or act in their company, in case it hurts their feelings or offends their dignity, or to act up to them in order to support their pose, we become strained by their society. They are costing us dearly in psychological energy.

The individual who is simple, who accepts themselves as they are, makes only a minimum demand on others in their relations with them. Their simplicity not only endows their own personality with unique beauty; it is also an act of real love. This is an example of the truth that whatever sanctifies our own soul does, at the same time, benefit everyone who comes into our life. (*The Passion of the Infant Christ*, p. 82)

✳   ✳   ✳

OUR BAPTISMAL VOCATION TO HOLINESS is intensified by God's creative life hidden within us this Advent, while at the same time more and more things are demanding our time and energy. More shopping. More travel. More planning. Pressure builds, and it is increasingly difficult to find quiet time for our Advent-life. As we brush elbows with more and more people who are more and more anxious for the season, we hear again our call to simplicity. The great mystery this Advent is that our personal holiness touches the lives of all those with whom we come into contact. When we are made holy as individuals, it is the whole world that reaps the reward. Being faithful to our baptismal vocation is an honest gift of self that we can share with our family and friends this Advent. Be faithful to the God who has called you by name. Other blessings will follow.

* * *

O MERCIFUL GOD WHO HAS CALLED US to be your own, help us this Advent to keep things simple and holy, for our salvation and the good of those whom we love.

Second Week of Advent

SUNDAY

Rest

The Parable of the Seed: "But as for that in the good soil, these are the ones who, when they hear the word, hold it fast in an honest and good heart, and bear fruit with patient endurance."

—Luke 8:15

T HE LAW OF GROWTH is rest. We must be content in winter to wait patiently through the long bleak season in which we experience nothing whatever of the sweetness or realization of the Divine Presence, believing the truth, that these seasons which seem to be the most empty are the most pregnant with life. It is in them that the Christ-life is growing in us, laying hold of our soil with strong roots that thrust deeper and deeper, drawing down the blessed rain of mercy and the sun of Eternal Love through our darkness and heaviness and hardness, to irrigate and warm those roots.

The soil must not be disturbed. Above all we must not disturb it ourselves by our own egoism. We must not turn it over and dig it up by anxieties and scruples. We must not shift it by fretting for a sense of personal perfection: to feel sinless that we may feel free from the pain of guilt and anxiety; to feel pure for the sake of vanity; to be reassured of the hidden presence of Christ in us by experiencing sensible consolation.

The seed must *rest* in the earth. We must allow the Christ-life to grow in us in rest. Our whole being must fold upon Christ's rest in us, as the earth folds upon the seed.

(*The Passion of the Infant Christ*, p. 15)

* * *

GOD'S WORD-SEED does not take root in barren places or scattered among thorns. In good soil, though, it bears fruit with patient endurance. We are dust, and to dust we shall return. But Jesus calls us to be more than dust. *Dust* is annoying and inconvenient, always out of place. Jesus calls us to be *soil*, which is quite another thing. Fill a pot with dust, and no plant would ever grow. Fill a pot with soil—dark, rich, earthy soil—and in time the seed will bear fruit. Soil lies in wait to receive the seed that comes quietly to life. So it is for us. Only when our "pots are settled" and we learn to be silent will God's Word-Seed spring to life within. This Advent, fold Christ deep into the soil of your heart, and indulge God a season to rest and grow in you. Grant God space to rest and lie peacefully within. All may seem quiet and still, but God's Word-Seed will take root and, in due season, we shall reap the harvest of new life.

* * *

O GOD OF LIFE, plant your grace and favor in us this Advent. Sow your seed. Teach us to rest and be still, and we will rejoice with you in life's new abundance.

MONDAY

Advent in Work

For it is God who is at work in you, enabling you both to will and to work for [God's] good pleasure.

—Philippians 2:13

E VERY WORK that we do should be a part of the Christ forming in us which is the meaning of our life, [and] to it we must bring the patience, the self-giving, the time of secrecy, the gradual growth of Advent.

This Advent in work applies to all work, not only that which produces something permanent in time but equally to the making of a carving in wood or stone or of a loaf of bread. It applies equally to the making of a poem and to the sweeping of a floor.

The permanency in it is the generation of Christ-life that outlasts time itself. It is eternal.

It is not only in work, in the realization of Faith, and in conscious prayer that we need the season of Advent; we need it in suffering, in joy, and in thought.

We need it in everything that is to bear fruit in our lives.

(*The Reed of God*, p. 36)

＊　＊　＊

WE DO NOT OFTEN THINK that God is truly at work in us, but surely this is true. The work of a Crafter and a Potter and an Artist who shapes and molds rough material—God colors and crafts us to be increasingly perfect and beautiful. God at work in us is a creative and dynamic process—one that is accomplished only in faith. Faith, because what we are fully to become has yet to be seen. Our true shape is coming to be, always in the Divine Artist's own image, always in process, always emerging. It is in this process that God has made us simultaneously always beautiful and always increasing in beauty. What is our own attitude toward work this Advent? Do we have time to uncover something beautiful in our work or in an ordinary day? Do we feel the Maker molding and shaping us? If we feel God nudging us, do we ignore it, or do we surrender? Is God's work our work this Advent?

＊　＊　＊

O CREATIVE, WORKING GOD WHO FORMS US IN BEAUTY, help us see patterns of your love in our ordinary, regular lives this Advent.

TUESDAY

The Wisdom of Childhood

For once you were darkness, but now in the Lord you are light.
Live as children of the light—for the fruit of the light is found in
all that is good and right and true.

—Ephesians 5:8–9

LL THE WAY to heaven is heaven," says Saint Catherine of Sienna, and this is a thousand times true of the heaven of spiritual childhood, because it means becoming, not any child, but the Christ Child who is the life and the heaven of the soul.

The ordinary experiences of adult life, offered to everyone if they will take them, are work, friendship, love, home, children, rest, old age, and death. Within these—varying and alternating—[are] poverty and riches, success and failure, forgiving and being forgiven, dependence on one another, illness and recovery, the illness and recovery of those whom we love, sometimes their deaths.

The experience at the core of every other, giving all the other experiences their significance, making them fruitful, is simply love. When we love, even the sufferings

that our love makes more acute throw us upon the heart
of God and teach us the wisdom of childhood.
(*The Passion of the Infant Christ*, pp. 84–85)

* * *

CHILDHOOD NAÏVETÉ is sacrificed on the altar of pain and
disappointment and, all too often, we end up callous,
hardened, and numb. Perhaps only in fits and starts,
childhood is beginning to be restored in us this Advent.
We are the children of the Light making ready for the
season of Light. The Light is already within us—growing
in secret places, storing up strength to burst forth in the
fullness of time. If we are silent this Advent, it is not
because we are numb or because we have nothing to say.
We are silent with full hearts and growing spirits—
making ready to shout forth with angels: "Behold, we
bring you tidings of great joy!" The time is not yet, but it
is coming. Let us continue to be still for a while longer,
to grow a bit stronger, to become yet a little more full
with the God who dwells within. And what a surprise it
will be to the "grownups" when our voices swell to honor
the Child-King with shouts of "Gloria!"

* * *

O GOD WHO RENEWS OUR YOUTH, stir up in us the
Light of your presence this Advent, so that
everything we say and do will be made brilliant with
your goodness.

WEDNESDAY

Every Ordinary Thing

"Are not two sparrows sold for a penny? Yet not one of them will fall to the ground apart from your Father. And even the hairs of your head are all counted. So do not be afraid; you are of more value than many sparrows."

—Matthew 10:29–31

C HRIST never goes away, never forgets, all day long, wherever you are, whoever you are, whatever you are doing. His whole heart is concentrated upon you.

He watches you with the eye of a mother watching an only child. He sees not the surface things, not the imperfections inevitable to human frailty, but the truly lovable in you, your dependence on him, your need of him. Does a mother love her child less because it has fallen and bruised itself? No, indeed; only, if that is possible, more!

What then must we do?

Listen. Be silent. Let Christ speak to you. Forget yourself, do not be self-centered, let him tell you how he loves you, show you what he is like, prove to you that he is real. Silence in your soul means a gentle attention to

Christ, it means turning away from self to him, it means looking at him, listening to him.

God speaks silently, God speaks in your heart; if your heart is noisy, chattering, you will not hear.

Every ordinary thing in your life is a word of God's love: your home, your work, the clothes you wear, the air you breathe, the food you eat, the friends you delight in, the flowers under your feet are the courtesy of God's heart flung down on you! All these things say one thing only: "See how I love you."

God asks only one thing, that you will let God tell you this, directly, simply; that you will treat God as someone real, not as someone who does not really exist. (*The Comforting of Christ*, p. 21)

* * *

WE ARE WATCHING, listening, and waiting this Advent. Mary watches her stomach swell as the Infant grows within her. The evenings are longer and, from the shadows, we await the dawn. It is also true that God is watching this Advent. God is watching us! God waits to delight us in simple things—to share beauty and love with us. In this way, our watching is not dull. We watch and we wait, but laziness is our only excuse for boredom. God sits in wait to overwhelm us at every turn—to surprise us with God's own great love that should astonish us with our every breath. In truth, we can never be completely still. In God's benevolent stewardship of creation, outside us the earth spins and the solar system whirls about, carrying us at astonishing speeds through the cosmos. Within, our hearts beat and our lungs pulse with air. As you keep watch this Advent, be mindful of the Holy One within who keeps vigil over you, even listening to your heartbeat.

* * *

O GOD WHO KEEPS WATCH OVER US, give us eyes this Advent to wonder in your constant care for us.

THURDSAY

Joy Must Be Allowed to Gestate

But we have this treasure in clay jars, so that it may be made clear that this extraordinary power belongs to God and does not come from us.

—2 Corinthians 4:7

A SEED CONTAINS all the life and loveliness of the flower, but it contains it in a little hard black pip of a thing which even the glorious sun will not enliven unless it is buried under the earth. There must be a period of gestation before *anything* can flower.

If only those who suffer would be patient with their earthly humiliations and realize that Advent is not only the time of growth but also of darkness and hiding and waiting, they would trust, and trust rightly, that Christ is growing in their sorrow, and in due season all the fret and strain and tension of it will give place to a splendor of peace.

The same with joy; we sometimes accuse young people of grasping joy and not realizing their blessings and not being made bigger and kinder and lovelier as they ought to be by all delight.

Joy must also be allowed to gestate.

Everyone should open their heart very wide to joy,

should welcome it and let it be buried very deeply in them; and they should wait the flowering with patience. Of course, the first ecstasy will pass, but because in real joy Christ grows in us, the time will come when joy will put forth shoots and the richness and sweetness of the person who rejoiced will be Christ's flowering.

We must never forget that it is the Holy Spirit who sows this Christ-Seed in us, and the Spirit of Wisdom, Light, Truth is given to us in countless ways.
(*The Reed of God*, p. 36)

* * *

CLAY SEEMS OUT OF PLACE in Advent. But this Advent we know that we are preparing for a great joy which shall be for *all people*—painted and glossy people, people accustomed to glitter and bows, and to the rest of us who are simple, clay pots—with more than our share of cracks and imperfections. We are simple people this Advent, both by nature and by choice. We are old in a world that celebrates the young. We are quiet when the world seems to shout, and often our faith calls us to speak up when others would prefer us to keep silent. Advent people can seem out of place—like clay pots hung on a fancy tree. Be aware of the Christ-Seed that is growing in you. Share with God what you consider to be your imperfections and limitations. Instead of being phony and adding glitter and bows, let God make your clay pot beautiful. It will take time, but it will happen. Be patient.

* * *

O GOD OF THE AGES, help us to wait in confidence this Advent.

Friday

Everything That We Do

Therefore Jesus had to become like his brothers and sisters in every respect, so that he might be a merciful and faithful high priest in the service of God, to make a sacrifice of atonement for the sins of the people. Because he himself was tested by what he suffered, he is able to help those who are being tested.

—Hebrews 2:17–18

W E KNOW what the Incarnation means to us, that God the Son, by becoming human, caught up our human nature into his, made each one of us one with him. He took our human nature for his own and gave us his. He experienced everything that we do, except sin, and he even took upon himself the guilt and punishment of sin.

He made himself subject to our limitations: to discomfort, poverty, hunger and thirst and pain. He knew fear, temptation, and failure. He suffered loneliness, betrayal, unrequited love, utter desolation of spirit, the sense of despair and death. He suffered all these things, and all the secret, incommunicable things known to each individual, which can never be told; and he overcame them all.

Christ has lived each of our lives. He has faced all our fears, suffered all our griefs, overcome all our temptations, labored in all our labors, loved in all our loves, died all our deaths.

He took our humanity, just as it is, with all its wretchedness and ugliness, and gave it back to us just as *his* humanity is, transfigured by the beauty of his living, filled full of his joy. So that no matter what suffering we meet, we can meet it with the whole power of the love that has *overcome* the world.

(*The Risen Christ*, pp. 1–3)

✳   ✳   ✳

GOD INTIMATELY and silently shares all of our secrets, no matter how hidden we may keep them from other people. God knows our hidden selves, and still God is pleased to be one with us. God rejoices in our private triumphs and shares the pain of our unspoken sorrows— all in complete and undisturbed solidarity with us. Christ's humanity remains the point of connection between our human lives—however seemingly petty and small—and the veiled, ineffable, and eternal life of God. This Advent we experience the indescribable mystery of God taking on our humanity, gaining for us a Great High Priest for all people and for all time. Angels can only wonder at the joy we know as daughters and sons of Eve: God has chosen to be one of us. Rejoice in your humanity! Celebrate your individuality! Know that God treasures you.

* * *

O GOD WHO COMES TO US IN ADVENT, help us
recognize our humanity as a gift that, with Jesus,
we share with you.

Saturday

Let Go

*For everything there is a season, and a time for every matter
under heaven:*

> *a time to be born, and a time to die;*
> *a time to plant, and a time to pluck up what is planted.*

—Ecclesiastes 3:1–2

F ROM COMING to know God as our Father through
our dependence, and as Father and Mother and
Lover through God's image in our souls, we learn
the simplicity, the humility and trust of children, but
only if we dare to love one another—if we accept the
loves that come to us in our lives, saying to each one as it
comes, "Be it done unto me according to your word,"
accepting the love and whatever its cost may be, the
responsibility of it, and the labor, the splendor of it, and
the sorrow.

As we grow old, we regain our likeness to little
children even outwardly. It is in surrendering to this that
we make our old age a thing of beauty and peace. We
become dependent on others. Our pleasures become
fewer and simpler, more and more like those of a child.
We let go, at last, of the struggles of the complicated

years that are over. The hopes that are no more, the
foolish little ambitions, the forgotten griefs.
Bereavements cease now to be loss, and change to the
anticipation of meeting our living dead again very soon.
Our values become true again; we distinguish as
unerringly as a child between the essential and the
nonessential. Our memory goes back to dwell again in
the morning of our life. Thus, when death comes, we are
able to accept this greatest of all our experiences with a
child's capacity for complete experience, and dying we
are made new.
(*The Passion of the Infant Christ*, pp. 85–86)

* * *

OUR LADY was a teenager that first Advent, Our Lord
still an Infant in her womb. Children are the focus of our
families and celebrations, and we increasingly wonder
how we who are old can fit into the season. This Advent,
we are called to an adult childhood. As we transition
through the seasons of life, we relearn the lessons of
childhood: being in awe over simple things, losing our
concern for power and control. To relearn how to be
content, simply to *be* who we are in the image of God.
After all, isn't that the example of Mary? In simplicity
and trust she yielded her heart, mind, and body to the
purpose of God. And that is the ultimate example of
Jesus: God who spent a term growing into humanity in
the womb of a young maid. This is who we are this

Advent—regardless of age or situation in life—replete in the dignity due one who is made in the very image and likeness of God.

✳   ✳   ✳

O GOD WHO EMBRACES ALL PEOPLE, teach us this Advent to grow old with dignity and confidence that you will always provide for us.

THIRD WEEK OF ADVENT

SUNDAY

Sacramental Life

Do you not know that your bodies are members of Christ?
—1 Corinthians 6:15

CHRIST USED THE FLESH AND BLOOD of Mary for his life on earth, the Word of love was uttered in her heartbeat. Christ used his own body to utter his love on earth; his perfectly real body, with bone and sinew and blood and tears; Christ uses our bodies to express his love on earth, our humanity.

A Christian life is a sacramental life, it is not a life lived only in the mind, only by the soul; through the bodies of men and women Christ toils and endures and rejoices and loves and dies; in them he is increased, set free, imprisoned, restrained. In them he is crucified and buried and rises from the dead.

Our humanity is the substance of the sacramental life of Christ in us, like the wheat for the host, like the grape for the chalice.

Christ works his love through material as well as spiritual things. Into his worship, following his own lead, the Church, his Church, brings material things, pure wax, flame, oil, salt, gold, water, linen, the voices of

people, the gestures and actions of people, our own souls and bodies—the substance of our flesh and blood. All this is consistent with the Incarnation, when Christ took the human nature of Our Lady to be himself.
(*The Comforting of Christ*, pp. 26–27)

* * *

GOD IS SPIRIT, and so are angels. Human beings (Christ included) are also flesh and blood—material, tangible, and concrete. Starting with the first Advent, and now throughout all eternity, God is flesh and blood in Christ. Immanuel—God *with us*. Immanuel—God *One of us*. In Christ God fully sanctified and drew the cosmos into Godself, sanctifying the world of touch and taste and smell. That is why it is only fitting that our common life as the people of God is also material—sacramental. Water, oil, bread and wine. These are the things that bind us to God and one another as Church. This Advent is truly a time for Sacrament. God invites you to touch, and taste, and smell. Listen to your body this Advent. Be aware of God's life growing—inside and outside. Stretch your senses and taste and see that the Lord is good.

* * *

O GOD WHO IN THE BEGINNING MADE ALL THINGS and who in time made all things holy with your presence, help us this Advent to see, to touch, and to taste your goodness.

MONDAY

Healing the Wounds of the World

Let your gentleness be known to everyone. The Lord is near. Do not worry about anything, but in everything by prayer and supplication with thanksgiving let your requests be made known to God.

—Philippians 4:5–6

T HE DIVINE INFANCY in us is the logical answer to the peculiar sufferings of our age and the only solution to its problems.

If the Infant Christ is fostered in us, no life is trivial. No life is impotent before suffering, no suffering is too trifling to heal the world, too little to redeem, to be the point at which the world's healing begins.

The way to begin healing the wounds of the world is to treasure the Infant Christ in us; to be not the castle but the cradle of Christ; and, in rocking that cradle to the rhythm of love, to swing the whole world back into the beat of the Music of Eternal Life.

It is true that the span of an infant's arms is absurdly short; but if they are the arms of the Divine Child, they are as wide as the reach of the arms on the cross. They embrace and support the whole world; their shadow is the noon-day shade for its suffering people; they are the

spread wings under which the whole world shall find shelter and rest.
(*The Passion of the Infant Christ*, pp. 87–88)

* * *

THE ARMS OF THE DIVINE CHILD grow increasingly long, stretching as they do through time and history. They bridge the gap between us and God. As the Divine Infant, God in Christ pulls close to us, and the Christ Child's arms hold us tight, near the very heart of God. Advent is a time for *presence*—God's manifested presence with humanity, and our presence with one another. This is a time for community, for bridging gaps and crossing divides. Learning to span generations and differences of culture and disposition is the greatest honor we can give the Christ Child, whose very life brought us into communion with God and unity with one another. This Advent forgive, forgive, and forgive. Draw others close to you. Draw yourself near to other people. In bridging gaps we draw nearer to God who this season draws ever closer to us.

* * *

O GOD WHO COMES NEAR, dwell in us this Advent. Transform suffering into joy, and disappointments into opportunities to forgive and be transformed.

TUESDAY

Saint Joseph: Quiet Strength

When Joseph awoke from sleep, he did as the angel of the Lord commanded him; he took her as his wife, but had no marital relations with her until she had borne a son; and he named him Jesus.

—Matthew 1:24–25

S AINT JOSEPH, the "just man" who was Christ's foster father, is an example of one who justly defends the defenseless. The grey-beard statues of him that we are used to, and drugged by, quite misrepresent his character. He was one who did violence to himself, who accepted hardship and danger, and renounced self to protect the little and the weak. In that mysterious anguish of misunderstanding of Our Lady, his one thought in the midst of his own terrible grief was how to save and protect her from the world. It fell to his lot to save the Divine Infant from Herod. He, like all those who cherish the life of an infant, had to give up all that he had in order to give himself. We know nothing of him after Christ's boyhood; all that is recorded of him is that he protected Our Lady in Advent, that he was the first to protect the unknown, unguessed Christ in another, and that he was the defense of the Infant Christ when he was defenseless and threatened by Herod. A just man and a strong man. Love was in him like the crystal in the rock. Justice is both the tenderest and the sternest expression of God's Fatherhood: it is the inflexible logic of Divine Love.

(*The Passion of the Infant Christ*, p. 109)

✷　✷　✷

OUR LADY was not so frail and demure that she could not have managed things on her own. In boldness and confidence her character was strong to accomplish God's will. Joseph's role was to support the unfolding of events with quiet strength. In spite of the gossip and wagging tongues of his neighbors, he married a woman who was already pregnant (and not by him!). He got them safely to Bethlehem, and when the Child came Joseph welcomed him, arranging for his temple sacrifice and his name. Whisking them to Egypt at the command of an angel and returning them home safely when, in yet another dream, God told him it was safe, Joseph showed profound devotion, availability, and great love. As a father he loved the Son that did not have his eyes—the Son of a Stranger. Take time to consider your life and your availability to God and others this Advent. Think about your capacity for sacrifice and for love.

* * *

O GOD WHO CALLS US TO LOVE AND TO SERVE, keep us faithful this Advent, so that like Joseph we may protect and nourish the Christ Child within all people.

SAINT JOSEPH, noble son of the house of David, pray for us.

WEDNESDAY

Act of Faith

Mary said to the angel, "How can this be, since I am a virgin?"
The angel said to her, "The Holy Spirit will come upon you, and
the power of the Most High will overshadow you; therefore the
child to be born will be holy; he will be called Son of God."

—Luke 1:34–35

TRUTH WOULD BE a very small and petty thing if it would fit into our minds.

If we took the sum total of all our moods, how seldom, if ever, would we be convinced by them that the Holy Spirit is within us and wishes to be at home in us. This is too mysterious a thing for us to accept through anything less than the Word of God.

We begin our seeking by making acts of faith in the presence of Christ in our own souls. Our Lady must have helped to form Christ in her soul by making acts of faith in his hidden presence within her. Sometimes, when she sat down in the cottage doorway after her day's work, she must have felt anew her amazement at the angel's salutation and have asked her own soul: "How can this thing be?" Could it be possible that the tiny little tunic that she was weaving was for *God?* That she had to guess the tiny size of God by the measure of her own littleness?

"How can this thing be?"

Acts of faith in the presence of Christ in us are the first active exercise in this contemplation. It is quite incredible to think that God is really present in me.

"My God, I believe that you are within me."

This act of faith brings peace: it silences the noise of distraction, the loud business of fear. It is the stilling of the waters.

It gathers our thoughts into a circle like a crown of flowers; it crowns us with peace.

(*The Reed of God*, p. 99)

* * *

WHEN WE MAKE AN ACT OF FAITH we are not trying to convince ourselves of some dubious reality, nor are we trying to make up God's mind. An act of faith is a verbal incarnation of truth. Saying it or praying it does not make it so, but because we *already believe* something is true we declare and affirm it to be true *for us*. In this way we come to own the truth. God's Spirit of Truth dwells within us and, in the Spirit, we become the friends of Truth. With even the simplest act of faith our capacity for discernment is honed and our faith is strengthened. This Advent, practice your gift of discernment. Awaken the Spirit of Truth that is inside of you. Say to God, "Here I am . . . let it be according to your Word." Listen, then follow.

* * *

O GOD OF BEAUTY AND TRUTH, show us how to walk in truth this Advent, so that your Word will come to fullness in us.

MY GOD, I believe that you are within me.

THURSDAY

Light Bearer

"You are the light of the world."

—Matthew 5:14

I T IS POSSIBLE to make a candle with very little wax and a lot of fat, but a candle made from pure wax is more useful and more fitting. The Church insists that the candles on the altar be made of pure wax, the wax of soft, dark bees. It is beautiful, natural material; it reminds us of the days of warm sun, the droning of bees, the summer in flower. The tender ivory color has its own unique beauty and a kind of affinity with the whiteness of linen and of unleavened bread. In every way it is fitting material to bear a light, and by light it is made yet more lovely.

The purpose for which human beings are made is told to us briefly in the catechism. It is to know, love, and serve God in this world and to be happy with God for ever in the next.

This knowing, loving, and serving is far more intimate than that rather cold little sentence reveals.

The material which God has found apt for it is human nature: blood, flesh, bone, salt, water, will, intellect.

It is impossible to say too often or too strongly that human nature, body and soul together, is the material for God's will in us. It is really through ordinary human life and the things of every hour of every day that union with God comes about.
(*The Reed of God*, pp. 4–5)

*　*　*

LIGHT COMES pretty inexpensively and maybe even too conveniently to us. With batteries in flashlights and the cool-to-the-touch fluorescent glow of chemical lights, Christ might well say to us anew: "You are the *fire* of the world." Fire is heat and combustion—fuel actively being consumed and transformed into energy. "Fire!" is a cry for attention, and a warning for anyone who is unprepared. That must be what Our Lord had in mind when he said, "You are the light of the world." We have grown accustomed to Advent being a season of light, but let's agree to make this Advent a season of fire. Be consumed by the energy that dwells and is growing within. Let it burn in you. Let God use fire to purify the cosmos through you and make ready the Way of the Lord.

*　*　*

O GOD WHO CONSUMES AND TRANSFORMS US in Advent, give us courage to blaze with the fire of your presence.

FRIDAY

A Procession of Life

Like abundant leaves on a spreading tree
that sheds some and puts forth others,
so are the generations of flesh and blood:
one dies and another is born.
Every work decays and ceases to exist,
and the one who made it will pass away with it.

—Sirach 14:18–19

L IFE IS RULED by a musical law. A procession of life
moves through the world; children, here yesterday,
are gone; the men and women they have become
are passing. The old people they will be vanish like
autumn leaves on the wind's drift, and the wind's drift
will seed the world. For as long as it lasts, the world will
be thronged with children, mature people, and old
people; for those who live, pass, life remains. Christ goes
on, the stream of life. War can kill living people; it can
destroy civilizations; it cannot end life. [Although]
humanity can destroy its own works, it cannot touch
God's.

The rhythm of the liturgical year is a natural
expression of our life in Christ. It is like the days and the

nights, like waking and sleeping, like the procession from childhood to resurrection.

At Christmas, Christ is born in us. At Passiontide he suffers and dies in us. At Pentecost the flame of the love of his Spirit is kindled in us. Advent returns, Christ with it, to his secret life in us, to be born into the world again. (*The Comforting of Christ*, pp. 30–31)

*　*　*

RHYTHM AND PATTERN mark the seasons of the years. Christ is renewed in us *every* Advent, but this *now* is our Advent. It would be impossible to relive last year. Next year God will be ready to do something new in us. *This* is our time. We will never meet this exact moment again. And *this* is the Advent where God dwells *in us*. Not in the person we were last year, not in the person of tomorrow that we might never become. God is *here*, God is *now*—arms open and ready to receive us. Jesus isn't waiting until December 25 to be born anew. Christ is present and full of new life *now*. God isn't biding time, waiting for heaven to love us and welcome us home. God and the fullness of God's love is already *here and now*. That is how we rejoice, even in the dead of winter and in the "not yet" expectation of Advent. Our God is the God of the eternal *now*—always ready to forgive, always ready to love. Are we?

* * *

O GOD WHO STANDS ALWAYS AT OUR SIDE, this Advent help us grasp you in every moment.

SATURDAY

Hats and Gloves

And all of you must clothe yourselves with humility in your dealings with one another.

—1 Peter 5:5

AWARENESS OF THE PRESENCE of the Divine Child in us draws us from every distracting and destructive preoccupation, such as self-pity, anxiety, irritability with other people, the morbidity which leads us to dwell more upon our own sinfulness than upon the beauty of God.

In the wonder of this awareness, we are able to accept the humiliation of being ourselves. The next act of faith is in Christ in other people.

It is very easy to believe in the indwelling presence of Christ in the souls of imaginary people, to believe in it in people whom we do not know. But it is very difficult to believe in it in the case of our own relations and our intimate friends.

Somehow it is difficult to believe that the Holy Spirit abides in people who are not picturesque. When we think of Christ in the workman, we think of him in a special kind of workman who wears an open shirt and is assisted in carrying the burden of social injustice by a truly magnificent physique. We do not think of him in the man who delivers the milk or calls to mend the pipes.

It is easy to believe in Christ in the refugee when he is on the road, easy to believe when the refugee mother arrives at an English port, with a shawl round her head and a baby in her arms. But how hard to believe in the presence of God in the same refugees when they have got good work, are housed and fed, and possess hats and gloves.

(*The Reed of God*, pp. 99–100)

* * *

IN SIMPLE, Advent humility, "the humiliation of being ourselves," we gain solidarity not only with the Son of God but also with our fellow human beings. Taking for ourselves the attitude which is Christ's, we have the eyes to recognize ourselves in the billions of brothers and sisters with whom we share the planet. Humility helps us look beyond the "hats and gloves," and through the skin, to the truth of the person who stands before us. And reflected in their eyes is more than a shadow of ourselves; it is our own mirror image—another glimpse of the incomprehensible image and likeness of God. Consider the image of God you have for yourself. Consider the image you have for your neighbor. Consider the image you have for the stranger. Now consider Jesus, the very

Pattern and Likeness of God. In humility, treasure each image as a gift from God.

✳ ✳ ✳

O GOD WHO COMES TO US IN THE THOUSANDS OF FACES we meet this Advent, help us to recognize ourselves in them, to welcome them, and so to welcome you.

FEASTS AND DAYS IN ADVENT

DECEMBER 8

Immaculate Conception - The Throne

"My soul magnifies the Lord,
     and my spirit rejoices in God my Savior,
for God has looked with favor on the lowliness of his servant.
     Surely, from now on all generations will call me blessed;
for the Mighty One has done great things for me,
     and holy is God's name."

—Luke 1:46–49

WHEN THE CHRIST CHILD once more reigns, his throne will be his mother's arms.
(*The Passion of the Infant Christ*, p. 113)

DEVOTION TO OUR LADY is the treasure of the Catholic Church. She has never ceased, all through the ages of Christianity, to foster this tender love for the Mother of God. As soon as children can walk, they walk to Our Lady's altar and put one more candle to shine among the countless candles at her feet, one more bunch of flowers from the fields is pushed into her hand or laid across her gilded shoes; and when the child is old and nodding before the altar, it is the same thing.

Every trifling thing is told to her and every great sorrow; she is the sharer of all earth's joys and griefs.

She is not wearied with our littleness; her smile comes down to us like a benediction through the sea of flickering candles, and she blesses our wildflowers withering at her feet. For each one of us is "another Christ"; each one, to Mary, is her only child. It is therefore not tedious to her to hear trifles that we tell her, to look at the bruises that we bring to her, and seeing our wound of sin, to heal it.
(*The Reed of God*, p. 121)

* * *

OUR LADY offers God her canticle of faith this Advent. As she watches her belly grow large with God, she becomes our Patron as we join her—waiting, watching, the Christ-Seed planted in us all. We learn from her how to foster the Christ-life within. As we keep vigil, Our Lady sits with us, listening with the patience of a mother, responding with the creative energy of a young girl. She teaches us that nothing is impossible with God. She tells us her story—the trials, challenges, and adventures that attend us when God dwells within. Christ rests in her womb, and Mary is transformed. We are invited into that love and transformation. Mary Immaculate first and fully bore Christ within. This Advent, find yourself caught up in Our Lady's love for Christ. Tell her your story. Let her delight in God's love for you.

＊　＊　＊

O GOD WHO GIVES US GRACE TO TRIUMPH OVER SIN, make us beautiful in purity and truth so that Christ may be fully formed in us.

PRAY FOR US, holy Mother of God.

DECEMBER 17

A Child at Rest

The wolf shall live with the lamb,
the leopard shall lie down with the kid,
the calf and the lion and the fatling together,
and a little child shall lead them.

—Isaiah 11:6

T HINK OF A CHILD asleep in her mother's arms; the abandon with which she gives herself to sleep can only be because she has complete trust in the arms that hold her. She is not lying asleep on that heart because she is worn out with anxiety. She is asleep there because it is a delight to her to be asleep there. The mother rests too. She rests in her child's rest. Her mind and body rest in her. Her head fits into the crook of her curved arm. Their warmth is mingled like the warmth of two softly burning flames. She rocks to and fro, and her rocking is unconsciously timed by her child's breathing. Rest is a communion between them. It is a culmination of content. On the child's part, utter trust in her mother; on the mother's part, sheer joy in the power of her love to sustain her life.

Such as this was the rest of God in the beginning of time, when God had created the world.

Our rest in a world that is full of unrest is Christ's trust in his Father; our peace in a world without peace is our surrender, complete as the surrender of the sleeping child to her mother, of the Christ in us, to God who is both Father and Mother.

(*The Passion of the Infant Christ*, pp. 17–19)

* * *

THIS ADVENT we learn to rest from the Divine Child, the One who rests in Our Lady. This Advent reminds us that we have been caught up in the ineffable and total love between God, who is our Parent, and Christ, the Only-Begotten of God—Light from Light. All of us now take part in this divine love and light that is bestowed, shared, and returned by us to God. The humanity of Jesus is our very real participation in the eternal relationship of mutual love within the Trinity: God, Child, and Spirit. It is not something that we can be robbed of—not something that can ever be taken away or lost. It is ours. It is a gift. It is our gift from God. It is in the gift of this Advent that we can truly find confidence, strength, and rest. Trust it. Draw warmth from the God who is warmed in Mary's womb. With Christ we are held close and share in the very life of God. Surrender.

* * *

O GOD WHO LIVES AND SHARES LIFE WITH US, give us warmth and rest this Advent. Help us surrender to your eternal love so that we may know peace without end.

December 18

The Power of Children

It is you who light my lamp;
the LORD, my God, lights up my darkness.
By you I can crush a troop,
and by my God I can leap over a wall.

—Psalm 18:28–29

IT IS IN OUR LADY that God fell in love with humanity. It is upon her that the Dove descended, and the love of God for humanity culminated in the conception of Christ in the human race. In the virginal emptiness of the girl, Mary of Nazareth, Christ was conceived; it was the wedding of God to a human child, and the wonder of it filled the earth for all time.

Christ's insistence on the power of children is very striking. Almost more than anything else in the gospel it proves that in God's eyes *being* something comes before *doing* something.

He sets a little child among his apostles as an example of what he loves. He says that heaven is full of children. Indeed, the Architect of Love has built the door into heaven so low that no one but a small child can pass through it, unless, to get down to a child's little height, they go in on their knees.

How consistent it is with the incredible tenderness of God that the Christ, the Immortal Child, should be conceived by the power of the Spirit in the body of a child. That a child should bear a Child, to redeem the world. Our Lady was, at the most, fourteen when the angel came to her; perhaps she was younger. The whole world trembled on the world of a child, on a child's consent.

(*The Reed of God*, pp. 10–11)

＊　＊　＊

AWAKEN YOUR IMAGINATION this Advent. God lights our lamp. With God we can leap over walls! What sheer delight and youthful energy the Divine Child gives us. Perhaps that is why God came to Our Lady when she was so young. Perhaps because of her youth, and certainly because of her faith, she truly believed in miracles—that with God a person could "leap tall buildings in a single bound." This confidence and trust is also God's gift to us this Advent. This season we have watched and waited, and the fulfillment of our vigil is near. We will shout the greetings of an angel choir to shepherds very soon. Is our voice in tune? Is our heart? Are our spirits full of God so that we are ready to jump over walls? Remember the best moments from your childhood this Advent. Recall a moment of imagination and wonder, and thank God for your gift.

*   *   *

O GOD WHO IS AT THE THRESHOLD THIS ADVENT, help us welcome and greet you with glad hearts.

December 19

No Room

. . . and laid him in a manger, because there was no place for them in the inn.

—Luke 2:7

W E ALL KNOW persons who are exaggeratedly house-proud, who concentrate on the neatness, cleanliness, beauty of their house, to the exclusion of its comfort. Their house is not a home, nothing must ever be left about, out of place. To come in with muddy shoes is a crime; it is a crime to disarrange the cushions! In such a house one can neither work nor rest; one is never at home, because it is not a home.

There are many people who are "soul-proud" in the same way. They spend their whole time cleaning up their soul, turning out the rubbish, dusting and polishing. Like the house-proud person, they become nervous, tired. There is nothing left in them to give, for they have wasted themselves on the silver, the curtains, the ornaments.

Christ wants to be at home in your soul. He will not go away and leave you if the house is chilly and uncomfortable; he loves you too much to leave you, but how often, how tragically often, he must say nowadays: "The Son of Man has nowhere to lay his head."

Christ asks for a home in your soul, where he can be at rest with you, where he can talk easily to you, where you and he, alone together, can laugh and be silent and be delighted with one another.

All this may seem daring, but it is true; it is the meaning of the Incarnation.
(*The Comforting of Christ*, p. 18)

* * *

THIS ADVENT has been about making room—room in our hearts, room in our bodies, room in our lives, to foster God within us. We have been attentive to priorities and dispositions, but if we have grown cold, then we have accomplished nothing. If ours is a piety that does not know how to laugh, a fierce humility that excludes the uninitiated, or even a consuming fire that burns but does not purify, then we have lost our way. We cannot have room for God if we do not have room for our neighbor. If a stranger knocks at two in the morning and we close the door—"no room at the inn"—we have truly had an encounter with God. But as we close the door, leaving the stranger outside, we have closed ourselves from an opportunity given to us by God to love and welcome another as God has loved and welcomed us. This Advent, think about making room. Find a place for spontaneity and a generous response.

Find a place to welcome the stranger and to throw back your head and laugh with God.

* * *

O GENEROUS GOD, help us this Advent to make room for a stranger in need, and show us your compassion.

December 20

Consolation and Delight

On that day the LORD their God will save them
*   for they are the flock of his people;*
for like the jewels of a crown
*   they shall shine on his land.*
For what goodness and beauty are his!

—Zechariah 9:16–17

THE CHRIST-LIFE in us follows a natural law of growth. All nature is made in the image of Christ's life, and Christ chose to submit himself to his own law; he was hidden in his mother's womb, like a seed in the earth, and there grew towards his birth. Our Lady could do nothing to hurry that birth, and she would not have wished to. She rested in God's will, in God's timing, in God's planning. Her mind was as big as the earth, as peaceful as the earth, as still as the earth in winter, and it covered heaven—heaven unfelt yet, unseen, growing towards the birth of Christ.

Now most of us tend to want to *feel* the presence of the indwelling Christ all the time; we want to experience continual sweetness in devotion, [and] our prayers are to be always breaking into flower within us. We are distressed because we know long periods when prayer

brings *us* no sweetness at all, and we forget in our distress that if we go on praying without any "consolation," we are giving *God* something God is due.
(*The Risen Christ*, pp. 106–107)

* * *

IT IS EASIER TO PRAY in times of grief and in times of joy. When emotions are high our spirits more naturally turn to God. Still, we know that a child grows and develops in the mother's womb whether or not she is consciously aware of it. Likewise, God abides in us regardless of our circumstances. In the first instance, where the child grows within the mother, it is the child who draws nourishment and warmth from her. God within us is quite the opposite. We are drawing our strength and vigor from God. This shared warmth is not something God endures or is hesitant to offer—just as the Incarnation was not a burden Christ was reluctant to accomplish. God delights in giving us life. Christ delighted in his mother's womb. It was not a punishment or a tomb for him—it is life for us, and to God we "are like jewels of a crown." Consider God's gift to you this Advent. Give yourself as a precious gift to God in return. Already you are God's delight.

* * *

O GOD WHO DWELLS IN US and bestows upon us beauty, grant us the grace to welcome your gift, and generously offer you the gift of ourselves this Advent.

December 21

The Fierce Beauty of Light

*On that day the root of Jesse shall stand as a signal to the peoples;
the nations shall inquire of him, and his dwelling shall be
glorious.*

—Isaiah 11:10

THOSE WHO SEEK are more aware than any others.
They observe every face; they look deep into
every personality; they hear every modulation in
the voice. They hear music and words and the sounds of
machinery, laughter, and tears with new hearing,
attentive ears. They hear and see and taste life in a new
way, with a finer consciousness, more analytically,
because they are searching, because truth and only truth
can ease their thirst; and with incomparably more
delight, because, in this seeking, searching, and finding
are one thing: everywhere and in everyone they find
what they seek.

But the finding is never complete. We can never
know God exhaustively or completely; and in this life we
cannot know even with the vision of the saints in
heaven. But we can sometimes know with knowledge
akin to the knowledge of the dead, for sometimes we

become so aware of the fierce beauty of God's light that it seems to be known because it is burning within us. (*The Reed of God*, p. 120)

*   *   *

WE HAVE DRAWN NIGH to the God who overshadowed Our Lady—the God who has caught us up in the love of the Divine Infant. The Desire of the Nations is about to be born, and the glory of heaven will fill the trough of a Bethlehem stable. And though we are soon to celebrate the dawn of his appearing, we know that when Mary holds him in her arms our trek has only just begun. Advent teaches us to seek and to wait, but this is the first step on a larger journey—one mile down a very long road. Even as the Desire of the Nations is set before our eyes, we know that God calls us to a new horizon. We are an Advent people. The Christ who is born for us calls his people forward. The Infant is the same Christ who empowers us to look ever deeper into ourselves and the world—to continually grow and be conformed to the image of God within us. Our minds are sharper now than they were at the start of this Advent, and it is our responsibility never to let them grow dull. Never forget the lessons of Advent. There is reason to rejoice in our growth, but we always have the task of birthing Christ in every moment of life.

* * *

O GOD OF TIME AND OF ETERNITY, we rejoice in your appearing this Advent. Help us attune our minds and hearts to your coming in this and every moment.

DECEMBER 22

A Seamless Garment

With joy you will draw water from the wells of salvation. And
you will say in that day:
> *Give thanks to the LORD,*
> *call on God's name.*
> *Shout aloud and sing for joy, O royal Zion,*
> *for great in your midst is the Holy One of Israel.*
> —Isaiah 12:3, 6

I T IS THE *Word* THAT IS MADE FLESH, the spirit of joy
and wisdom and love. So where the spirit is at home
in a human creature, and Christ born of his life is
manifest, there must be a grace of living which touches
every detail of life. Our minds must be quickened; we
must see the world in wonder and reverence; we must be
conscious that privations, pain, and weariness of the
body are prayer; but that so, too, are the pleasures and
labors of the body.

Body and soul together give glory to God. The
sharper the capacity for sorrow and joy, the greater the
hallowing; the subtler the delicacy of the daily life, the
surer is Christ proved in it. In office or home or hospital,
prison, barracks, or church—anywhere at all where men

and women are—the mystery of the Incarnation can bear fruit in bodies and souls all day and night, too.

The crippled child who is patient, lying still; the urchin who dances in the gutter to the barrel organ; the soldier in battle; the clerk in the office; the woman dusting her home: in all of them the Word is made flesh and, if we will, we can behold him in his glory, Who is dwelling among us.

Christ laid hold of the world with his human hands; he took it to his human heart; with his body he wed himself to it. Our life is the response of the bride.

"Lift up your hearts."

"We have lifted them up unto God."

We have thought about the simplicity of the things Christ chose to use, but the simplest of all and the first essential was the humanity of Mary of Nazareth, in whose flesh the Word was made flesh.

Christ has laid his humanity upon us—a seamless garment, woven by a woman, single and complete, beautiful like the lilies of the filed, passing the glory of Solomon but simple as the wildflowers; a wedding garment worn to the shape of his body, warm with his life.

(*The Reed of God*, pp. 66–67)

* * *

WHEN CREATION lifts the Christ Child to God, we are lifted up as well—one holy offering to God. From the lofty heights of God's favor we see that we have been made beautiful in simplicity this Advent, now robed in the garment which is Christ. God has planted salvation deep within the well of our humanity, and it is drawn forth this Advent in celebration. The Only-Begotten is born for us, and our royal voices shout: "Triumph!" This moment is full of grace and favor. This is our salvation.

✳   ✳   ✳

O GOD WHO LOOKS DEEP WITHIN and transforms our darkness into light, shine the light of your face on all people this Advent.

December 23

Wait

You know what time it is, how it is now the moment for you to wake from sleep. For salvation is nearer to us now than when we became believers; the night is far gone, the day is near.

—Romans 13:11–12

T OO MANY ANXIOUS CHRISTIANS today think that their efforts to preach and teach and enter into outward activities can do more to save the world than the surrender of their souls to God, to become Christ-bearers.

They believe that they can do more than Our Lady did, and they have no time to stop to consider the absurdity of this. They fear that if the world goes on hurling itself into disaster, as it seems to be doing now, Christ's kingdom may be defeated. This is not so; Christ has given his word that he will be with and in his "little flock" until the end of the world. However dark our days may seem to be for Christianity, they are not so dark as the night following the crucifixion must have seemed to be to the apostles. For that night Christ had already prepared them. He told them to *wait*: to wait for the coming of the Holy Spirit. He told them to wait simply in the city; not to run away, not to make plans of their own, not to be troubled, but to wait, with his mother among them, for the coming of the Comforter.

God does not change; the preparation for the coming is the same.
(*The Risen Christ*, pp. 109–111)

*   *   *

OUR WAITING is about to bear fruit, and still the world hurls on the brink of disaster. Our Lady is great with child and even she is not spared hardship—traveling from Nazareth to Bethlehem. She will not give birth in her home surrounded, as she might well have preferred, by friends and family. The whole world is great with child, and still we are not prepared for childbirth. Humanity, pregnant and full with the power of God's indwelling, wanders in lonely wilderness, preparing to give birth on violent street corners and in dark alleys, making infant cribs lean with poverty, hunger, and war. We bear the secret of God's love within us. We have long felt the stirrings of the Life within—the kicks and leaps of God in us yearning to be born. And God will come— poor and hungry, a voiceless stranger. There is a Christmas tree in our home, our lights are strung and glowing, our pantries are full, and we are ready to entertain family and friends—but have we made room to feed and welcome the Stranger who comes unannounced?

*　*　*

O GOD WHO HAS FILLED US WITH GOOD THINGS, show us your compassion this Advent. Teach us humility and courage.

December 24

Christmas Eve Morning

Stars and Snow

*"Joseph, son of David, do not be afraid to take Mary as your wife,
for the child conceived in her is from the Holy Spirit. She will
bear a son, and you are to name him Jesus, for he will save his
people from their sins."*

—Matthew 1:20

S NOW FALLS, and once again the wonder of
childhood is upon us. At first a few separate flakes
float down slowly, one by one; then more, faster
and faster, filling our eyes with dazzling, dancing
whiteness. The movement is more mysterious because it
is silent: dancing, wild dancing, with no sound, like
voiceless singing. If it made even the tiny tap of hail it
would seem to fall into our world, but the silence is
absolute; it is we who are walking in another world, a
world in which we are ghosts. The falling flakes touch
our faces with unimaginable lightness and melt on the
faint warmth of our blood, at once elusive and intimate.

There is no one who does not sometimes return to
their childhood, walking in the snow, back to the
enchanted garden, where the Snowman stands at his

slightly tipsy angle, with his mouth of red berries and his battered top hat. There we meet Hansel and Gretel again, and the Snow Queen with her ice-blue eyes. We walk in the footsteps of King Wenceslaus to the poor man's cottage, and come suddenly upon Saint Francis, the little poor man, making his snow bride. And Francis leads us to the crib and shows us the Divine Infant sleeping amidst stars and snow.

(*The Passion of the Infant Christ*, p. 29)

* * *

THE VERY FIRST WORD out of the Christmas angels' mouth is: "Do not be afraid." We see an Infant, a beaming Mother, some oxen in a stable, a snowflake and a star, and we are not afraid. We also know that God has set more before us than what is understood by the senses. There truly is no reason for us to fear, but faith also understands that the pulse of God's own life and power lends its rhythm to the comfortable symbols of Christmas. This tiny town of Bethlehem holds the court of heaven. The ox and the ass behold the unfolding and full display of God's salvation. The Infant in swaddling clothes is the Christ of God. So it is fitting that our minds also find time for snowmen with red berry mouths and Hansel and Gretel and images of our own childhood. These are also gifts of God, and the real beauty and power of faith lies veiled in the optimism and imagination of children—those who do not need to see to believe. After all, we can only stumble upon Saint

Francis and the Child Jesus—it comes as a surprise and a gift. We cannot control it or master it. We can only surrender, be surprised, and let it fill us with wonder.

✳   ✳   ✳

O GOD OF HIDDEN WONDER, this Christmas expand our minds and stretch our imaginations so that we may wonder at your appearing.

JESUS, meek and humble of heart, come! We long to see your face.

DECEMBER 24
CHRISTMAS EVE AT MIDNIGHT

Dream Come True

*And she gave birth to her firstborn son and wrapped him in
bands of cloth, and laid him in a manger.*

—Luke 2:7

ONLY LOVE is incarnate. Goodness is natural
because the Divine Child, who submitted
himself to the law of his Father's love, has made
it so. Christ subjected himself to the law of the seed in
the earth, to the law of rest and growth. He was "one of
the children of the year," growing through rest, secret in
his mother's womb, receiving the warmth of the sun
through her, living the life of dependence, helplessness,
littleness, darkness, and silence which, by a mystery of
the Eternal Law, is the life of natural growth.

His life in the womb was measured, like those of all
the other children of the year, by a certain destined
number of cycles of darkness and light, by the rising and
setting of the sun so many times, by the rise and ebb of
so many tides, by a certain counted number of beats of
his mother's heart.

Who can think of the mystery of the snowflake, its loveliness, both secret and manifest, its gentleness, the moving lightness of its touch, the humility of its coming, and not think of the birth of the Infant Christ?
(*The Passion of the Infant Christ*, p. 42)

* * *

THE LIFE OF GOD WITHIN US now issues forth. For countless generations God had fueled the imaginations and dreams of our ancestors, but tonight God comes forth in a gush of water and blood *for us*. The Infant cry of Christmas reminds us that God is real—that our salvation is accomplished by One of us, the Christ who is born. We have watched and waited, and the day is come. The clock and calendar that have accompanied us through Advent are now set aside. Seasons have passed and time flows away, but this Christmas we enter eternity. The Lord of the universe is wrapped in baby clothes, and the angels of God attend him in a manger. Gentleness. Moving lightness. The humility of his coming. This is the dream-time: the moment when dreams come true. Legends of animals talking and Santa Claus all fit somehow into Christmas magic—but this is even better. The Christ is our dream come true. This is the wholeness of God's love made flesh. He is beautiful, and he is ours. Come, let us adore.

* * *

O GOD WHO SHARES OUR DREAMS, we welcome the gift of your very Self this Christmas. Help us to welcome you, and to sing.

JESUS, Joy of Angels, have mercy.

FEASTS AND DAYS IN CHRISTMAS

DECEMBER 25

CHRISTMAS DAY

The Way of Peace

By the tender mercy of our God,
*   the dawn from on high will break upon us,*
to give light to those who sit in darkness
*   and in the shadow of death,*
*   to guide our feet into the way of peace.*

—Luke 1:78–79

HOW SMALL AND GENTLE his coming was. He came as an infant. The night in which he came was noisy and crowded; it is unlikely that, in the traffic and travelers to Bethlehem, the tiny wail of the newly born could be heard.

God approaches gently, often secretly, always in love, never through violence and fear. He comes to us, as God has told us, in those whom we know in our own lives. Very often we do not recognize God. God comes in many people we do not like, in all who need what we can give, in all who have something to give us; and for our great comfort. God comes in those we love. In our fathers and mothers, our brothers and sisters, our friends

and our children. Because this is so we may not be content ever to love with only *natural* love. We must also love everyone with a *supernatural, sacramental* love. We must love Christ in them with Christ's love in us. It would be well if those seeking perfection ceased trying so painstakingly to learn how *not* to love and learned instead how to love well.
(*The Passion of the Infant Christ*, p. 46)

✳   ✳   ✳

THE TINY INFANT guides our feet in the way of peace, and we must learn to be content with that being a quiet, ordinary way. The quiet stillness of Advent is now shattered with the demanding cries of an Infant. Yet even this cry of heaven was not heard above the din of a busy city. The world did not stop spinning when he was hungry (although it might have). The ox and the ass must have been inconvenienced by the events going on around them—shepherds in from the countryside pressing in and looking on in wonder. And when the shepherds did return, walking back to the fields to tend to their flocks, their hearts were full and there must have been a bounce in their step. Returning to work, they walked in the way of peace. The night before, they had heard the announcement of angel choir. In the darkness of that night they had been led to see the salvation of Israel with their own eyes. Still, the next morning they returned to work. They did not go on retreat or take a holiday. They went back to work—back to the ordinary.

However, their lives had been transformed and their feet were renewed to walk in the way of peace. Let's follow them.

*   *   *

O GOD WHO RENEWS US THIS CHRISTMAS, help us keep track of the ordinary, even in the midst of celebration, so that our feet will never stumble in the way of peace.

JESUS, radiant Sun of Justice, have mercy on us.
JESUS, Son of Mary, grant us peace.

DECEMBER 26

The Out-going of Advent

All who heard . . . were amazed at what the shepherds told them. But Mary treasured all these words and pondered them in her heart.

—Luke 2:18–19

ADVENT WAS A FOLDING upon the life growing in our darkness. Now the seeking is a going out from ourselves. It is a going from our illusions, our limitations, our wishful thinking, our self-loving, and the self in our love.

Yet this outgoing begins gently: it has something of the quality of Advent. Before the Divine Child leaves us, we are allowed to experience the loveliness of his indwelling presence. Therefore, when he has gone, the longing to find him again will be stronger than anything we may meet in the seeking; stronger than the fear which makes us want to remain locked up in our own limitations. No matter how hard the way, it will be in some measure sweet to us, and we shall take it, not as a path along which we are driven, but as one whose attraction we cannot resist, because we know that on it we shall discover him.

Where must we seek?
Everywhere—in everyone.
  How must we seek?
  With faith and courage and limitless love.
  First of all, by faith.
(*The Reed of God*, pp. 97–98)

* * *

IN ORDER TO EMBRACE the Infant Christ at Christmas, we
have gently let go of Advent. Take a quiet moment to
reflect upon all you have done and thought and prayed.
The Christ-Seed has sprung forth from us and has begun
to bloom. The secret we had been keeping close within
us in Advent is now public, and the Judean countryside
is now buzzing with the news. The quiet, still Word has
now been spoken. From now on, Mary's Child and our
Infant Christ belongs to strangers as much as to us—to
the shepherds and onlookers and very soon to wise men.
Our Lady ponders all these things, and so her watching
and waiting continue. She hears the shouts of glory and
praise of God, and shares the excitement of the angel-
struck shepherd-folk. Things are different for us now.
The light from our Advent vigil now shines and draws
crowds. Our Lady keeps us connected to Advent, but the
way of the shepherds point us forward—to seek and to
share what we have seen.

* * *

O GOD WHO GIVES US TIMES OF QUIET and times of action, abide in us this Christmas so that all people may be filled with the joy of your presence.

DECEMBER 27

Mind Reflecting Love

That disciple whom Jesus loved said to Peter, "It is the Lord!"
—John 21:7

PERHAPS OUR LORD took so young an apostle as John into his motley little company in order that he should be still a boy when he took Our Lady home. Perhaps, too, his very special love for John may have had something to do with the future, in which Christ foresaw John giving his mother no time to grieve after his crucifixion.

After a fashion, she had been crucified with her son; and Mary's longing for Christ is beyond our knowing. But faith and a boy in the house could make life very full. It is moving to think of her once more baking the kind of cakes she knew boys like; once more patching and darning, and sewing buckles on sandals; once more talking of the things that interested the boy and being a companion to his thought. And how fitting it was that the companion of John's thought should be Our Lady. For John's was the mind of crystal in which all the fires

of love reflected, and Mary's was the mind of the girl
who sang the Magnificat.
(*The Reed of God*, p. 125)

*   *   *

CHRISTMAS IS THE TIME for us to celebrate, to rise up from
the quiet vigil of Advent, and to "gird up our loins."
Saint John helps us direct our thoughts from the Crib to
the life and teaching of the One who so recently has
been born. We know that the Infant whom the angels
sang will soon speak words that will challenge our hearts
and our minds. Soon he will come into his own and call
fishermen to his side, daring to eat with sinners. He will
work wonders, teach Wisdom, and know friendship and
love and betrayal. And when he is lifted up on the Cross,
Saint John will console and care for Our Lady. The same
John whom Jesus so dearly loved, and who, that dawn
soon after Our Lord's resurrection, first recognized the
Risen Lord. Even from the fishing boat, John's sharp eyes
saw that it was Jesus talking to them from the lakeshore.
"It is the Lord!" he cried, and Peter jumped in and swam
to where Christ had prepared them all breakfast. The
eyes of the young—the sharp eyes of young Saint John
who recognizes the Lord from afar and cries out—let
those be our eyes this Christmas.

* * *

O GOD WHO RENEWS THE STRENGTH OF OUR YOUTH, give us eyes to recognize you and the courage to journey with you this Christmas.

GOOD SAINT JOHN, beloved of the Lord, pray for us.

December 28

Holy Innocents, Martyrs

Any Child Might Be Christ!

When Herod saw that he had been tricked by the wise men, he was infuriated, and he sent and killed all the children in and around Bethlehem who were two years old or under . . . Then was fulfilled what had been spoken through the prophet Jeremiah:
> *"A voice was heard in Ramah,*
> *wailing and loud lamentation,*
> *Rachel weeping for her children;*
> *she refused to be consoled, because they are no more."*

—Matthew 2:17–18

HAD THOSE LITTLE BOYS grown to manhood, God alone knows what their individual destinies would have been. But whatever they might have been, they would certainly be long forgotten. They would have no part in us now, no comfort for our sorrow, no redeeming for our sin, no beauty for the lifting of our hearts, no lesson to sustain our hope. Their Eternity would not have been as it is, the purest joy that God, even God, can give, unimaginable, unending delight in God.

Baptized in blood, those little children were among the first comers to heaven. Fittingly they, with their tiny

King, are the founders of the Kingdom of Children. We celebrate their feast with joy; it is the most lyrical in the year. They reach down their small hands to comfort every father or mother bereaved of a child. They are the first who have proved that the Passion of Christ can be lived in a tiny span by little ones. They are the forerunners of the magnificent sanctity of our generation, the "spiritual childhood" of Saint Theresa of Lisieux. The tears that dried on their faces two thousand years ago in Jerusalem have the redeeming power of Christ's tears today. Each one of those infants is the first Christ Child of the Incarnation, the first of the first generation to call the Mother of God blessed.

Herod ordered the children to be killed because he was afraid that any one of them might be Christ.

Any Child might be Christ!—the fear of Herod is the fear of every tyrant, the hope of every Christian, and the most significant fact of the modern world.

(*The Passion of the Infant Christ*, pp. 95–97)

* * *

BECAUSE GOD IS REAL and truly enfleshed in Christ, there is a weight his presence has on the world. The weight is borne by us in differing degrees, but each of our lives is different because of God's presence. The promise of universal hope—"Any child might be Christ!"—bore down heavily upon the children of Bethlehem of Judea. There, the Son of God drew his first breath, and breathing the very same air were the first Christian martyrs—infants too young even to speak a word in their defense. The presence of Christ is costly because the promise of Christ is priceless. Let it also be justice.

✳︎   ✳︎   ✳︎

O GOD OF EQUITY AND COMPASSION, teach us justice and mercy this Christmas.

HOLY INNOCENTS AND MARTYRS of God, pray for us.

DECEMBER 29

Love

As servants of God we have commended ourselves in every way:
through great endurance, in afflictions, hardships, calamities . . .
as having nothing, and yet possessing everything . . . In return—I
speak as to children—open wide your hearts also.

—2 Corinthians 6:4,10,13

THERE IS NOTHING MORE MYSTERIOUS than infancy; nothing so small and yet so imperious. The Infancy of Christ has opened a way by which we can surrender self to him absolutely, without putting too much pressure on our weak human nature.

Before a child is born the question which everyone asks is, "What can I give them?" When the child is born, the child rejects every gift that is not the gift of self; everything that is not disinterested love. The child rejects everything but that because that is the only thing the child *can* receive.

Disinterested—not one-sided—love. One-sided love is never a consummated love, never a communion. It is a disintegrating, destructive thing. But disinterested love, objective love without conscious self-interest, is as near to perfection as anything human can be.
(*The Passion of the Infant Christ*, p. 47)

* * *

A CHILD'S life is full of messy, inconvenient, selfless
moments that adults would find embarrassing and
humiliating. What self-respecting, human dignity can
there be in diapers and bibs? These are adult judgments,
and all that an infant can recognize and receive is love.
That is the standard for dignity—love is the hallmark of
compassion. That is how we can hear the message of
Saint Paul this Christmas—our very male, celibate, ex-
convict, haggard and bruised, begging-for-bread witness
to love and spiritual childhood. In love and childhood
we are open to the voice of others. We make room to
allow the voice of a man with no wife or children teach
us about love. We listen to the silent testimony of a
Divine Child, proclaiming him the Wisdom of the Ages,
even while he nurses at his mother's breast. This is love
and the openness we have as the children of God. Be
confident and trust it.

* * *

O GOD WHO SPEAKS WISDOM IN SILENCE and calls
Light from darkness, open for us the doors of
endless possibilities this Christmas.

DECEMBER 30

HOLY FAMILY
(SUNDAY IN THE OCTAVE OF CHRISTMAS)

Warm Woolen Garment

But Zion said, "The LORD has forsaken me,
my Lord has forgotten me."
Can a woman forget her nursing child,
or show no compassion for the child of her womb?
Even these may forget,
yet I will not forget you.

—Isaiah 49:14–15

NOW, MOST WONDERFULLY, we can learn God's care for us by searching our own hearts. The father and mother within us is only the faint image of the Father and Mother in God. God is the Father and Mother whose heart never sleeps; whose hands never lift from their works that they have made; who has numbered the hairs on our heads; in whose humanity we are clothed as in a warm woolen garment; in whom we live as in our home; who is our food and our drink, our shade in the heat, our comfort in sorrow, our healing when we are wounded, our light in darkness.

The Christ-life in us, the Infant Christ of our soul, is the Only-Begotten Son in the hands of God. It is God's creative love that has given us life, that sustains life, that is our life.

God it is who says, "Can a woman forget her infant?" (*The Passion of the Infant Christ*, p. 57)

* * *

THIS CHRISTMAS we recognize that we are children who share our infancy with the Divine Infant. Christmas teaches us that God is at home with us. Not visiting, not passing through—God is *at home.* Shoes come off, pretenses are left behind, beds are unmade, our hair is out of place, and dirty dishes fill the sink—nevertheless God is at home. We are one in the family of faith, sharing our small planet as together we hurl through space. This is our home, and these are our brothers and sisters. We have no excuse to be irresponsible, selfish, or unjust, but we also have the invitation to rest, to find warmth, and to seek comfort in God our Mother and Father. We are not alone. God journeys with us, and we journey together. Smelly socks and dirty diapers are part of our family history as much as sacraments and cathedrals. Recognize that God is pleased to share *every* part of you.

* * *

O GOD WHO EMBRACES US THIS CHRISTMAS, show us your care in every moment of our lives, and teach us all how to live together in peace.

SAINT JOSEPH, protect us.
HOLY MARY, Mother of God, pray for us.
INFANT JESUS, save your people.

December 31

The Little Nations

May all kings fall down before him,
all nations give him service.
For he delivers the needy when they call,
the poor and those who have no helper . . .
From oppression and violence he redeems their life;
and precious is their blood in his sight.

—Psalm 72:11, 14

JUSTICE CONSTRAINS US to insist openly on the rights of the little nations, to do penance for the sins against them in our own lives, to give all that we can for their relief.

For in them Christ will be born again; that lovely truth which haunts Herod down the ages will be realized—any Child may be Christ. In any humble, frustrated life, Christ may be born. It may be that in the divine heart of an old peasant, who has lost all his sons, the Divine Son will be born, and the old man will be made anew, and his life will renew the earth. It may be that in the life of some forgotten prisoner, the Incarnation will take place, and there, secretly, in swaddling bands, the country's life will begin again. It may be that in the soul of a hungry little child the Light that illuminates the whole world will begin to shine in darkness.

When Christ, born secretly in the little nations, in the martyr countries of the world, is recognized and worshipped openly, those countries will be clothed in their own particular heritage of beauty once more and receive back their own individual character.

Then the meek will inherit the earth, the earth that has nourished them like a mother; that has flowered for them and given them their bread; the earth on which their homes were built; the earth that has been watered with the blood of their sons and in which their sires sleep.

The gentle one, in whose power the meek will inherit the earth, will be the Child-Christ, crowned as King. (*The Passion of the Infant Christ*, pp. 111–12)

✳   ✳   ✳

CHRISTMAS HAS BEEN A TIME when wars have been paused to allow the faint whisper of peace to quiver over the body politic. But what peace has ever come from among nations that gives honor to the divine heart of an old peasant, or honors the soul of a forgotten prisoner or hungry child? Yet this is the peace of Christmas—quite unrecognizable from the peace that is won by missiles or the threatening rattle of sabers. And we must ask ourselves: "When the meek inherit the earth, what will our portion be?" To be meek and humble of heart—what does that mean for us? What would we have to change to accomplish such a thing for ourselves? Do we need to wait for a famine to strike or for war to break out before we challenge ourselves to be heroic? How desperate does a situation have to be before we have the courage to act on our faith? Must we wait for Christ's return before we redeem ourselves from violence?

* * *

O GOD WHO IS CROWNED WITH PEACE AND JUSTICE, stir up in us the fire of commitment this Christmas, so that we will accomplish your will with courage.

JANUARY 1

Solemnity of Mary, Mother of God

A great portent appeared in heaven: a woman clothed with the sun, with the moon under her feet, and on her head a crown of twelve stars. She was pregnant and was crying out in birthpangs, in the agony of giving birth. And she gave birth to a son, a male child, who is to rule all the nations with a rod of iron.

—Revelation 12:1–2, 5

HIS COMING was foretold on David's strings of gold, cried aloud on the tongues of prophets cleansed by fire. But when he came the Word of God was less than a whispered word, muted to the sound of tears and tuned to human ears. It was simply the beating of a virgin's heart.

Christ asked Mary of Nazareth for her human nature. For her littleness, her limitations, flesh and blood and bone, five senses, hands and feet, a human heart.

He who was invulnerable asked to be able to feel cold and heat, hunger and thirst, weariness and pain. He who had all things and had made all things asked to be able to be poor and to labor with his hands and look with wonder at the wildflowers. He who was wholly sufficient to himself asked Mary to give him a heart that might be broken.

Mary answered "yes." To make his body she gave her body, for his humanity, her humanity. The first utterance in this world of the Word of God was less than the infant's wail that it waxed to, it was the heart of Christ beating in a girl's heart.
(*The Comforting of Christ*, p. 23)

✳   ✳   ✳

THE "YES" OF OUR LADY and the cries of her childbirth ring out through faith's history. Her voice is one that we acknowledge and recognize as one of our own. The maid of Nazareth confidently offered her mind, will, and body to God in her youth. She is the same whose voice sung the Magnificat to the Holy One of Israel, and who cried out weeping at the foot of the Cross. She who was pained at Christ's birth was herself pierced through the heart at his death. And she who was filled with the Spirit of God at Christ's conception was filled anew with the same Spirit at Pentecost. She is the first and the fullest witness to God in Christ, and her "Yes" resounds through the centuries as our common voice of assent to the will and the working of God in our midst. The heart of her compassion courses through the whole people of God, and our faith is forever bound to her consent. Behold, the handmaid of the Lord.

* * *

O GOD WHO MADE MARY THE MOTHER of our
Redeemer, help us to follow her example this
Christmas and always to say "Yes" to you without
counting the cost.

VIRGIN gentle in mercy, pray for us.
QUEEN raised up to glory, pray for us.
HOLY MARY, Mother of God, pray for us.

JANUARY 2

Making Life a Liturgy

For I am convinced that neither death, nor life, nor angels, nor rulers, nor things present, nor things to come, nor powers, nor height, nor depth, nor anything else in all creation, will be able to separate us from the love of God in Christ Jesus our Lord.

—Romans 8:38–39

THE OFFERING of the body in prayer is at the heart of life and includes everything in our daily life, so that it radiates out into the world we live in, giving the majesty of liturgical action to our work and leisure, our eating and sleeping and speaking and moving; giving to our simplest act the redeeming power of the offering of Christ's Body, and making it both sacrifice to God and communion with humanity.

We shall carry this idea into the world, into the kitchen and the office, making life a liturgy, so that through it those prayers that Christ wishes to be made unceasingly will be made, regardless of our mood, and in tranquility.

Now it will be in the power of the Trinity and the majesty of the Liturgy that we do the things which before seemed only effort and boredom. Every step to the office, or to and fro in the home, will be a counted, preordained step, like the numbered steps in the sanctuary. We shall kneel in sorrow for sin and in adoration, whether we kneel to scrub the floor or to fasten the little child's shoe.

In its simplest terms the way to restore our souls in the prayer of the body is to slow down our pace to the pace of the Liturgy, to prune our minds to its huge simplicities.

(*The Risen Christ*, pp. 70–71)

* * *

LITTLE PEOPLE, quiet moments, intimate and personal concerns—these share the stage as God works our salvation. The Liturgy reminds us of this: bread and wine and water and oil are set apart and shared— communicating the presence of God who transforms the mundane into the miraculous, time into eternity. And not just at Mass, the source and summit of our life, but also in the quiet masses of our daily life, where body postures and voices communicate to other people. In our own homes and in the cathedral of our own hearts, we are priests and shepherds. A mother and father are as bishops to their children, and we are all responsible to one another in the great conclave of humanity. Our steps are holy, our eyes and ears have been opened, and our hands and voices are consecrated to God. We offer our daily work, and we share the sacrament of ourselves with everyone we encounter throughout the day. We are holy, and God would make our simple holiness the salvation of the world.

✳ ✳ ✳

O GOD WHO HAS ASSURED US OF YOUR PRESENCE and called us to be holy, help us conquer pettiness and bickering so that we may offer a pure sacrifice this Christmas.

JANUARY 3

Suffering

For this slight momentary affliction is preparing us for an eternal weight of glory beyond all measure, because we look not at what can be seen but at what cannot be seen; for what can be seen is temporary, but what cannot be seen is eternal.

—2 Corinthians 4:17–18

G OD'S PRESENCE or absence is known by the effect of suffering on us, especially by the effect of the small sufferings of every day, such as the "slights" which literally corrode those who try to endure them in their own strength. But in those in whom Christ abides, it is Christ who suffers every humiliation; for them there are no psychological scars, the Humility of Christ clothes them in his Majesty and crowns them.

It is not *what* is suffered that redeems and heals; it is *who* suffers. One tear of Christ's could redeem the world: all the tears of the whole world that are not his are of no avail to comfort one child.

What matters is not that we suffer, or that we suffer a little or a lot, but that Christ suffers in us. That Christ suffers whatever we suffer. Not that our lives are small or are lived on a heroic scale, but that they are lived by

Christ in us. Therefore, our way to share in the world's healing, to mitigate the world's suffering, is simply to foster and cherish the Infant Christ in our souls.

Because the Christ in us is the Infant Christ, it is in our littleness that we are stretched to the size of the Cross; it is in our helplessness that we are crucified in him.

(*The Passion of the Infant Christ*, p. 94)

✳   ✳   ✳

THE DIVINE INFANT is small by choice and design, not by necessity. God chose to accomplish great things in human littleness. Salvation was won for us in the confines of flesh and blood, space and time. There is no time when we feel so helpless and confined as when we suffer. Pain and disappointment press down upon us, wrapping us in iron bands. At such times, it is not enough for us to console one another with platitudes. "Time heals all wounds" is not an acceptable answer for one who suffers. Real pain makes time irrelevant, for when we suffer, a moment is as a lifetime. Time does not heal, but Christ does. Time cannot heal because time has not suffered. The Infant Christ heals because he has known pain, shares *our* pain, and stands with us in our suffering. There is no platitude, no answer, no solution to offer. What Christ can and does offer is God's *presence* in our suffering. God is with us—even when we suffer. Apart from that there is no meaning. Let us be present, then, to those who suffer.

*   *   *

O GOD WHO IS ONE WITH SUFFERING, apply your soothing, healing balm to all who anguish, are lonely, or in pain this Christmas.

January 4

Light of the World

In him was life, and the life was the light of all people. The light shines in the darkness, and the darkness did not overcome it.

*—*John 1:4–5

B Y THE LIGHT OF A STAR, the first who sought for him, after Mary, were guided. They followed a star, seeking the light of the world, expecting to find a newly born king, someone visibly predestined to be a great leader. They found a peasant's newborn baby in a stable. And they worshipped him.

Christ is the Light of the World; the sun which shines upon everything; gives color to everything; heals and gives life, light, and heat; the warmth that goes down deep to the root of the tree and discovers the tiniest seedling in the darkness and feeds it and draws it up into the day. But it is not only as the light of the sun that Christ wishes to be seen but also as the little candle burning in the house, a candle in a dark room.

"I am the Way," he said. And when we read the Gospels we begin to recognize what this means to those who are seeking for him in human beings. For everywhere, in everyone, there is some moment or experience of his going on, all through time. On earth he was little, joyful, afraid, sorrowful, tempted, loving, a failure, a king—everything that we can be, except a sinner; and even in sinners he is there in the Tomb, lying dead, awaiting and desiring resurrection. (*The Reed of God*, p. 112)

* * *

LIGHT IS THE ENERGY that powers life. The stars inspire poetry, and the sun warms the earth to melt even the harshest of winters. And Christ is that, and more. The Christ-Seed that has taken root in Advent and flowered in us this Christmas is now the engine that energizes us to live lives that are faithful to our experience of growth and transformation. Does the fire of God's life twinkle in your eyes this Christmas? Do you still see with the Infant's eyes—full of imagination, wonder, and joy? Our spiritual childhood has been renewed, and God has restored us in beauty. Have we already forgotten? Take some time today to reflect. The Christmas rush is past. Are you tired? Do you feel hollow now that the Christmas season is drawing to a close? If so, remember the lessons of Advent. A hollow in us can be made a space for God to dwell and grow large in us. If you have space, share it. God will make it radiant.

*   *   *

O GOD OF LIGHT, we open our lives to you again this Christmas. Renew us, fill us, and lead us in mercy by the fire of your Spirit.

January 5

The Mystical Body

*Jesus' prayer to God: "As you have sent me into the world, so I
have sent them into the world. And for their sakes I sanctify
myself, so that they also may be sanctified in truth . . . Father, as
you are in me and I am in you, may they also be in us, so that the
world may believe that you have sent me. The glory that you have
given me I have given them, so that they may be one."*

—John 17:18–19, 21–22

THE MEANING of the Mystical Body of Christ is that
Christ lives in all Christians. The practical result
of this, for us, is that now on earth the whole of
Christ's life is always being lived; the things that
happened to him on earth are happening to him now in
his members. The things that he did on earth he is doing
now through us. In us are all his needs as a human being:
his need of food and drink and sleep; of sympathy,
friendship, comfort, and love; his need of solitude, his
need to adore.

No single one of us can lead all of his life; to do so
would be to live all the lives of all the people who live
now, who ever have lived, and who ever will live. The
experience of even one human emotion is sharply

restricted in us by the narrowness of our hearts. Even a child, whose capacity is so much bigger than that of a grown-up person, soon falls asleep, worn out, if he is visited by great joy or grief, and it is a matter of every day to see a child laugh while tears are wet on his cheeks.

Each one of us can only live a fragment of Christ's life at one time, perhaps one moment of it or one incident or one experience. But through our communion with one another in Christ, through our oneness with one another because of his one life in us all, we make up what is wanting in one another and are whole; and in us all, as one body, Christ's whole life is lived. (*The Reed of God*, p. 104)

✳   ✳   ✳

IN OUR GLOBAL CONTEXT it should be easy for us to draw ourselves out of the narrow existence of our own lives, and to begin to see ourselves as part of the complex tapestry woven by everything that lives. It is liberation to understand that our lives are lived in the context of everyone else's life. The weight of humanity does not rest on any one of us, the faith of the Church does not reside in any one person, and our personal failures and shortcomings are more than compensated for by the gifts and abilities of our neighbor. This is community. This is Church. We trust that someone will cover our backs, we rely on the kindness of strangers, and we know that we are not in this alone. Put aside suspicion and prideful independence. The Body of Christ is interdependent. We need one another. We are each other's gifts from God. This is our holy communion. Together we are one, and together we are made the glory of God.

* * *

O GOD WHO CALLS US INTO FELLOWSHIP AND UNITY, teach us compassion this Christmas, and gather us in.

FEASTS AND DAYS IN EPIPHANY

January 6

The Epiphany of the Lord

Shepherds and Kings

"Master, now you are dismissing your servant in peace,
according to your word;
for my eyes have seen your salvation,
which you have prepared in the presence of all peoples,
a light for revelation to the Gentiles
and for glory to your people Israel."

—Luke 2:29–32

G OD CHANGES EVERYTHING.
God sends us to where *God* wants us to be;
among those whom *God* wishes to be among; to
do that which *God* wishes to do in our lives.

God brings to the Bethlehem of our lives those
people to whom God wishes to show the Infant Christ in
us; those who are to give us something for him, just as
God brought whom he would to Bethlehem: animals,
angels, shepherds, and kings. Unlikely people, proving
that, though there are distinctions between different
kinds of people in the world, when they come into
Christ's presence there is to be no distinction, no
selection; the rich and the poor, the ignorant and the

learned, the laborer and the king, must kneel together to the Infant Christ.

With all the ingenuity and all the sincerity in the world we cannot arrange our lives as God can to ensure that we give the Infant Jesus *his* necessity in us, not our goods or our thoughts of him, but ourselves.

Our humanity is to clothe him. Our love to be the four walls that shelter him. Our life to sustain him. (*The Passion of the Infant Christ*, p. 128)

✳   ✳   ✳

TODAY THE INFANT CHRIST is made manifest for all people. The Light now extends to every distant shore and penetrates even the thickest of walls politic. Today Our Lady lets go of her Son a little more. Christ issued forth from her body, leaving the secret place where their lives were intimately shared. In Advent, only Mary could feel his arms and only she knew when the heels of his feet pressed against her. The circle widens at Christmas. The Divine Infant receives the gaze of the ox and the ass. Soon, shepherds from the hillside are invited into the Mystery by angel voices in choir singing: "Glory!" Now at Epiphany, the wise men appear from afar. King Herod is given notice. The star had proclaimed his appearing, and now the nations are come to honor the one true King whose realm knows no boundaries of space or time. Our Lady receives them. The wise ones kneel in homage to the Child couched, at rest at her bosom. They open their coffers and precious gifts are bestowed upon the

Infant Christ. The Light has come for every nation to behold. The heavens declare him, the earth receives him, and humanity welcomes him, for he comes to us. Our salvation has drawn nigh, nursing and on the knee of a maiden.

＊　＊　＊

O GOD WHO COMES TO ALL PEOPLE, draw us to you this Epiphany. Enlighten us and show us how to offer you the gift of ourselves.

JESUS, Splendor of God, have mercy on us. Show us the beauty of your face.

JANUARY 7

The Light of Christ

But in these last days God has spoken to us by a Son . . . He is the reflection of God's glory and the exact imprint of God's very being, and he sustains all things by his powerful word.

—Hebrews 1:2–3

OUR CONCEPTION OF CHRIST colors our whole life; it informs everything that we touch with its spirit; it makes us what we are.

We become what our conception of Christ is: God made us in God's own likeness, but we have an extraordinary power of changing ourselves into the likeness of the idols we make, of those caricatures of God which we set up on the altars of our egoism and worship.

In the degree of our falseness of our conception of God, we restrict and narrow our interests and sympathies; we grow in intolerance and hardness or in a flabbiness which turns to a rot of sweetness like a diabetes of the soul.

In the degree of the truth of our conception of God, our minds grow broader, deeper, and warmer; our hearts grow wiser and kinder; our humor deeper and more tender; we become more aware of the wonder of life.

Our senses become more sensitive; our sympathies stronger; our capacity for giving and for receiving greater; our minds are more radiant with a burning light, and the light is the light of Christ.
(*The Reed of God*, pp. 85–86)

* * *

OUR ADVENT CONTEMPLATION and our Christmas wonderment have lent our minds insight and our hearts wisdom and love. These truly are the Light of Christ. The Light in which we walk is moderate and kind, tempered by forgiveness and understanding. It would bathe the world in its gentle glow and wash away the darkness. But things are still lurking in the shadows—staring us down from the darkness with eyes of fire. History that haunts us, pain that has not healed, wrongs we have suffered that have not been let go: these dim the Light when they are not confronted, when we do not allow Christ's Light to shine in the darkest corner of our life and down the most dangerous alley of our cities. Light's glory is to dispel darkness. Christ has illumined you with wisdom and the fire of his presence. It has been sparked and kindled in you. Let it blaze.

* * *

O GOD, OUR GOD, who is a consuming Fire, this Epiphany dispel our darkness with the fire of wisdom and understanding.

JANUARY 8

Advancing in Wisdom

When they had finished everything required by the law of the Lord, they returned to Galilee, to their own town of Nazareth. The child grew and became strong, filled with wisdom; and the favor of God was upon him.

—Luke 2:39–40

CHRIST WAS AND IS completely human, as well as being completely God. He went to collect the eggs in the farmyard and noticed how the hen gathered her chicks under her wings. He watched the wheat grow, from the thin green spear to the reaping, probably giving a hand with the harvest and hearing the farmers talk of the tares in the grain, the sheaving and threshing and the rest.

He watched his mother baking bread, fascinated as any child by seeing it rise. He watched her bottling wine, patching old garments, sweeping her house, lighting the lamps; he went with her to draw water from the well.

He talked, as boys love to do, to the shepherds and to the fishermen down on the shore. He listened enthralled to the stories of shepherds who had given their lives for their sheep, and the stranger stories of the sea, told by the fishermen who were out all night in their boats.

It was not only with his mind that Christ grew in knowledge; his emotions, too, responded to everything around him, so that when he came to teach the crowds, the images that he used were memories of his childhood and his mother's home, but the detached observations of the absorbed little boy were now charged with the burning love of the grown man.

He was leaven and light; he was bread and wine and living water; he was the good shepherd and the mothering bird.

It is not enough for us, if we live in Christ, to try to imitate what he did. We must also acquire his personality and grow to the maturity of our Christhood through the means by which he grew to his maturity of manhood, so that the trifling things of our experience, transitory by themselves as the fall of a rose, become charged with eternal meaning by the ray of his light.
(*The Risen Christ*, pp. 51–53)

* * *

THE IMITATION OF CHRIST is difficult enough, but we have been called to *become* Christ. In *becoming*, there is no room for hypocrisy or half-hearted commitment. We are with him, or we are against him. Growing and always increasing in beauty and perfection, we are ever more aware of God's strength and new life pulsing in us. Commitment to Christ is not dreary or dull. It is fascination and wonder, awe and abundance. It is life itself. Live!

* * *

O GOD OF WISDOM, grow in us this Epiphany and fill our minds with truth and our hearts with the wonder of your great love.

January 9

Humility

So we, who are many, are one body in Christ, and individually we are members of one another . . . Live in harmony with one another; do not be haughty, but associate with the lowly; do not claim to be wiser than you are.

—Romans 12:5; 16

CHRIST cannot act in conflict with himself. There is in him the flow and sweetness of order and harmony, perfect as pure music, and it is clear that his mind and heart are doing what his hand is doing. In the tiny threadlike capillary in his little finger flows the blood that sweeps through his heart.

We may, however, have what seems to us a very small part, to live out our lives among the humblest, to act far more in obedience than on our own initiative. Well, it was the fingertips of Christ that carried the love of his heart to the wounded world; the tips of his fingers that touched the blind eyes and sick bodies; the tips of his fingers that were the contact between his mind and broken human nature.

We may be the fingertips of the Mystical Body of Christ, working among the little and lowly because they most need his healing, and through us he can best heal.

This, then, is humility, to know ourselves as part of the whole Christ.
(*The Comforting of Christ*, pp. 3–4)

＊　＊　＊

WE CAN NEVER LISTEN to our own heartbeat without feeling some strong sense of identity. The heartbeat of a stranger is never quite the same as the "thump-thump" we hear from a stethoscope that is pressed cold against our chest. And so it is with the Mystical Body of Christ—God's ownership of humanity. In Christ, God's ear is tuned to hear the rhythm of every human heartbeat, and it is our task in humility to recognize our part in that mystery which is greater than ourselves. We imitate Our Lady who had a unique claim on Our Lord, but who also released her Son to share him publicly with all of us. Even as a Child, he was offered by Mary to shepherds and kings for worship. So, too, God's love for us is not exclusive or unique to us as individuals—God's love and favor are things we must learn to share. As individuals, we are each loved completely by God, but equally so is the stranger. God hears every human heartbeat.

＊　＊　＊

O GOD WHOSE LOVE IS GREATER THAN WE CAN IMAGINE, this Epiphany turn our lives and interests into service for our sisters and brothers.

JANUARY 10

Charged with Wonder

"Prepare the way of the Lord,
make his paths straight.
Every valley shall be filled,
and every mountain and hill shall be made low,
and the crooked shall be made straight,
and the rough ways made smooth;
and all flesh shall see the salvation of God."

—Luke 3:4–6

I T IS A GREAT PART of our Christ-life to increase joy in the world, just as it is. First of all in our own lives, for joy must be a reality, something as deep and still and pure as water hidden in a well, under the ground. The forced smile of the amateur Christian is a blasphemy.

We cannot increase joy unless we "put on" Christ's personality and our own joy is actually his. People driven by the fiend of vanity who roams abroad—not seeking whom he may devour but trying "to spread a little happiness," seeking with whom they may interfere— know nothing of true joy.

First of all its increase must begin in ourselves. We must grow in wisdom as Christ did, by deepening our understanding of the sacramental life through the very substance of every day—until there is nothing we see or touch that is not charged with wonder for us, though it is something as familiar as bread on the table; and there is nothing that we do, though it be no more than filling a glass with water for a child, which does not sweep the loveliness of God's sacramental plan through our thoughts, like a great wave of grace washing them clean from sin and the sorrow that is inseparable from it.

Then we can increase joy through compassion, even where there is incurable suffering, for if we even want to put on Christ's personality, we shall radiate his light, and he is the light which shines in darkness, which darkness cannot overcome.

(*The Risen Christ*, pp. 60–61)

* * *

OUR VOCATION is to level mountains, to raise the valley and the gorge, and to make level plains and straight paths; a huge task. Engineers would call for dynamite and mighty engines and powerful machines. John the Baptist shows us another way. With justice, water, and the Word of God, he makes ready the way of the Lord. On the shores of the River Jordan, a prophet tells us that the ax is ready to chop down the tree, and the Lord will appear with a winnowing fork to clear the threshing floor. If we have two coats, we must share one. Soldiers, tax collectors, the simple, and the wise hear alike: "Bear the fruit of repentance!" Our Epiphany light is increasingly put to the test. We are at a serious business, raising valleys and pulling down mountains. But John the Baptist teaches us that our dynamite power is not the choking sulfur of explosive self-importance; it is the gentle gift of water that displays the power of God.

*   *   *

O GOD OF STRENGTH AND OF REFRESHMENT, prepare us this Epiphany for your appearing. Shower us with the waters of righteousness and cleanse us from sin.

JANUARY 11

A Man in Love

"The Spirit of the Lord is upon me,
because [God] has anointed me
to bring good news to the poor.
[God] has sent me to proclaim release to the captives
and recovery of sight to the blind,
to let the oppressed go free,
to proclaim the year of the Lord's favor."

—Luke 4:18–19

I T WAS THE *Word* THAT WAS MADE FLESH. Not only did he take our sorrows to himself, but he gave the delight, the happiness that *he is,* to our humanness. No man ever enjoyed life as much as he did. He gathered up the color, sound, touch, meaning, of everything about him and united it all to the most exquisite sensitiveness, the most pure capacity for delight.

Most people know the sheer wonder that goes with falling in love, how not only does everything in heaven and earth become new, but the lover becomes new as well. It is literally like the sap rising in the tree, putting forth new green shoots of life. The capacity for joy is doubled, the awareness of beauty sharpened, the power to do and enjoy creative work increased immeasurably. The heart is enlarged; there is more sympathy, more warmth in it than ever before.

This being in love increases a person's life, makes them potent with new life, a life-giver; from it comes all the poetry, music, and art in the world. Human beings, made in the image of God, must also make the image of God's own love. We make songs and tunes and drawings and poems; children's stories, fairy stories; jewels, dances, and all else that tells the story of our love long after our heart is dust.

Christ on earth was a man in love. His love gave life to all loves. He was Love itself. He infused life with all the grace of its outward and inward joyfulness, with all its poetry and song, with all the gaiety and laughter and grace.

(*The Reed of God*, pp. 62–63)

* * *

IN CHILDHOOD, Jesus must have drawn some of his imagination and knowledge of Scripture from Our Lady. They both were filled with absolute confidence in the promises of God, and neither was shy or reluctant to declare their confidence. Mary sang the bold Magnificat, and here Jesus has the words of Isaiah now upon his own lips. Jesus reading the words of Scripture, rolling up the scroll, sitting down and proclaiming himself to be the Fulfillment and Ancient of Days. Eyes glued to him, ears straining to gather every word—Jesus, son of Joseph, has come to his people. And with what imagination and drama! No games or childish pranks, but the scene is rife with his confidence in God and innate knack to capture and inspire an audience. This Jesus stands apart, full of confidence and joy inspired by love. Allow his confidence, imagination, and grace to inspire you to act boldly. Astonish the crowd with your love. Let loose your tongue and proclaim the year of the Lord!

✳ ✳ ✳

O GOD WHO LIBERATES THE CAPTIVES, this Epiphany free us from self-doubts and insecurities. Give us the freedom to speak words of poetry and to love.

JANUARY 12

Secrets of Nazareth

[Jesus] came to Nazareth, and was obedient to them. His mother
treasured all these things in her heart. And Jesus increased in
wisdom and in years, and in divine and human favor.

—Luke 2:51–52

O F COURSE CHRIST did not create the things that
he made in Joseph's shop. They were the result
of hard work, of patiently acquired skill, just
like any other artisan's work. The miraculous element is
that *God* could have to work to make anything—that he
should have to get his skill like any other lad in the
workshop—measure, calculate, learn to sharpen his
tools; that a man, whom he had created, should teach
him to make the first long, clean cut with the saw, and
how to run the plane smoothly along the sweet-smelling,
newly cut wood. It is the strange thing that, though the
Son of God spent the longest part of his life making
things out of wood, there is nothing that he made left in
the world. There is no record of even a passing reference
to one of his works.

If only this world could boast of a stool, a chair, a
wooden bowl, a yoke for oxen, or any single thing at all,

made by the hands of God, when God was a workman!

How beautiful, too, that treasure would be; what proportion, exactitude, what finish and purposeful beauty it would show. But there is nothing at all to show for Christ's working life!

Did anyone value his work? Did his customers pick fault with it, haggle over the price of it, beat him down? All these things are hidden in the silence that keeps the secrets of Nazareth.

(*The Risen Christ*, pp. 28–29)

* * *

THOSE HIDDEN, secret years of Jesus are cause for much speculation. All we know for certain is that he was obedient to his parents and grew in the favor of God and with the people who knew him. Of course he labored, and of course he knew his share of skinned knees, personal failures, and secret life that belongs to every clumsy, growing boy. And perhaps we know nothing of the specifics of this "hidden" life for that very reason—so we are reminded that Jesus is truly One of us. His childhood was *our* childhood—good and bad. He knows the same successes and defeats that we all learned on the schoolyard and at our first job. What Jesus took from his experience was the beauty and the power and the splendor of childhood. He kept a boyish imagination and a child's compassion for every stray kitten and lost dog. When Jesus became an adult, these became part of his bold character and willingness to risk reputation and dignity in order to love—to risk loving even a sinner.

* * *

O GOD WHO RISKS EVERYTHING TO LOVE, this Epiphany show us compassion that does not count the cost, and teach us to share it without hesitation.

January 13

The Baptism of the Lord
(Sunday following Epiphany)

No Outward Sign

The next day John saw Jesus coming toward him and declared,
"Here is the Lamb of God who takes away the sin of the world!"
—John 1:29

T HERE IS NO OUTWARD SIGN of the miracle that is taking place. Office workers are bending over their desks, mothers working in their kitchens, patients lying quietly in hospital wards, nurses carrying out the exacting routine of their work of mercy, craftsmen at their benches, factory workers riveted to their machines, prisoners in their cells, children in their schools. In the country, farmers rise with the sun and go out to work on the land until sunset; the farm wives are feeding, milking, churning, cooking for their men and their children. Everywhere an unceasing rhythm of toil, monotonous in its repetition, goes on.

To those inside the pattern of love that it is weaving, it seems monotonous in its repetition; it seems to achieve very little.

In the almshouses and the workhouses, old people, who are out of the world's work altogether at last, sit quietly with folded hands. It seems to them that their lives add up to very little too.

Nowhere is there any visible sign of glory. But, because in every town and village and hamlet of the world there are those who have surrendered their lives, who have made their offering daily, from the small grains of the common life, a miracle of Love is happening all the time, everywhere. The Holy Spirit is descending upon the world.

Upon the world that seems so cruel, mercy falls like summer rain; upon the world that seems so blind, light comes down in living beams. The heart of humanity that seems so hard is sifted, irrigated, warmed; the water of life floods it. The fire and light of the Spirit burn in it. The seed of Christ-life, which seemed to have dried up, lives and quickens, and from the secret depths of our being the Divine Life flowers.

(*The Passion of the Infant Christ*, pp. 142–143)

* * *

THE HOLY SPIRIT is descending upon Christ, and through him the Spirit descends upon the whole world. The water flowing from the hand of John the Baptist inaugurates the season of God's great favor. The secret life of Advent is made manifest. The celebration of Christmas is fulfilled. The Epiphany Light now shines before the face of every nation. The Word-Seed is now lush and green, and the quiet pattern of life is now baptized in fullness—grace upon grace. In the water stands the grown Infant of Bethlehem. The heavens break open for him, and the time of God's Anointed One has come. Long ago, when Our Lady was only a maid and not yet married, the Spirit overshadowed her and embraced humanity in her womb. Today that same Spirit again embraces humanity—embraces us and all creation—warming us with the life that is God. We have journeyed long, and God has sustained us. Surely we are loved.

✳   ✳   ✳

O GOD WHO BATHES CREATION with the water of salvation, warm us with your Spirit and your mercy so that we will green and flourish and bear fruit.

LAMB OF GOD, have mercy on us.
GOD OF PEACE, pour out your Spirit, and renew the face of the earth.

And the Word became flesh and lived among us,
and we have seen his glory,
the glory as of a father's only son,
full of grace and truth.
From his fullness we have all received,
grace upon grace.

—John 1:14; 16

✳ ✳ ✳

Christ does not change; the preparation for the coming of the
Spirit is the same today as two thousand years ago, whether
it be for the rebirth of Christ in one soul that is in the hard
of winter, or for the return from the grave of Christ, whose
blood is shed again by the martyrs. The preparation is
the same: the still, quiet mind, acceptance, and remaining
close to the Mother of God, resting in her rest while the Life
of the world grew within her towards the flowering
of everlasting joy.
(The Risen Christ, p. 111)